The Far Right in America

This book collects Mudde's old and new blog posts, interviews and op-eds on the topic of the US far right, ranging from right-wing populists to neo-Nazi terrorists. The main emphasis of the book is on the two most important far right developments of the 21st century, the Tea Party and Donald Trump. Primarily aimed at a non-academic audience, the book explains terminology, clarifies the key organizations and people and their relationship to (liberal) democracy.

Cas Mudde is Associate Professor in the School of Public and International Affairs at the University of Georgia, USA, and Researcher in the Center for Research on Extremism (C-REX) at the University of Oslo, Norway.

Routledge Studies in Extremism and Democracy

Series Editors: Roger Eatwell, *University of Bath*, and Matthew Goodwin, *University of Kent*.

Founding Series Editors: Roger Eatwell, *University of Bath* and Cas Mudde, *University of Georgia*.

For more information on this series visit: https://www.routledge.com/politics/series/ED

This new series encompasses academic studies within the broad fields of 'extremism' and 'democracy'. These topics have traditionally been considered largely in isolation by academics. A key focus of the series, therefore, is the (inter-)relation between extremism and democracy. Works will seek to answer questions such as to what extent 'extremist' groups pose a major threat to democratic parties, or how democracy can respond to extremism without undermining its own democratic credentials.

The books encompass two strands:

Routledge Studies in Extremism and Democracy includes books with an introductory and broad focus which are aimed at students and teachers. These books will be available in hardback and paperback. Titles include:

The Populist Radical Reader
A Reader
Edited by Cas Mudde

The Far Right in America
Cas Mudde

Routledge Research in Extremism and Democracy offers a forum for innovative new research intended for a more specialist readership. These books will be in hardback only. Titles include:

38. The Darkest Sides of Politics, II
State Terrorism, "Weapons of Mass Destruction," Religious Extremism, and Organized Crime
Jeffrey M. Bale

The Far Right in America

Cas Mudde

LONDON AND NEW YORK

First published 2018
by Routledge
2 Park Square, Milton Park, Abingdon, Oxon OX14 4RN

and by Routledge
711 Third Avenue, New York, NY 10017

Routledge is an imprint of the Taylor & Francis Group, an informa business

© 2018 Cas Mudde

The right of Cas Mudde to be identified as author of this work has been asserted by him in accordance with sections 77 and 78 of the Copyright, Designs and Patents Act 1988.

All rights reserved. No part of this book may be reprinted or reproduced or utilised in any form or by any electronic, mechanical, or other means, now known or hereafter invented, including photocopying and recording, or in any information storage or retrieval system, without permission in writing from the publishers.

Trademark notice: Product or corporate names may be trademarks or registered trademarks, and are used only for identification and explanation without intent to infringe.

British Library Cataloguing in Publication Data
A catalogue record for this book is available from the British Library

Library of Congress Cataloging in Publication Data
A catalog record for this book has been requested

ISBN: 978-1-138-06387-7 (hbk)
ISBN: 978-1-138-06389-1 (pbk)
ISBN: 978-1-315-16076-4 (ebk)

Typeset in Times New Roman
by Taylor & Francis Books

Contents

Acknowledgments ix
Preface xi
Abbreviations xiii

1 Definitions: The various shades of the US far right 1
2 A short history of the far right in America 4
3 The Tea Party paradox 9
4 Wisconsin's Sikh massacre: The real danger 11
5 America's new revolutionaries 15
6 America's election and the Tea Party 19
7 Is the revolution eating its children?: The Tea Party between AstroTurf and grassroots 23
8 The Green Scare: Why Islamophobia is the new Red Scare 27
9 The Trump phenomenon and the European populist radical right 31
10 The power of populism?: Not really! 35
11 Is the GOP a far right party? 39
12 Will Donald Trump transform the (far) right in the US? 43
13 Donald Trump: The Great White Hope 46
14 A talk with Cas Mudde on American and European populism 52

15	The far right has arrived ... and it could take Washington!	56
16	The revenge of the losers of globalization?: Brexit, Trump and globalization	58
17	Stop using the term "alt-right"!	61
18	Why is American political science blind on the right eye?	63
19	Did Trump really hijack the GOP?	67
20	The latest Trump (and GOP and media) fiasco in nine points	70
21	Brexit, Trump, and five (wrong) lessons about "the populist challenge"	74
22	Keeping it real in Trump's America	79
23	The far right in a Trump world	82
24	Donald Trump is an American original	85
25	Trumpism: Normal pathology or pathological normalcy?	88
26	Donald Trump and the silent counter-revolution	94
27	What's the matter with America?: Trump and the multidimensionality of politics	99
28	Did Trump prove US political science wrong?	103
29	The politics of nostalgia	108
30	2016 and the five stages of liberal denial	111
31	We are thinking about populism wrong: And it's costing us	114
32	The Trump presidency: The far right in power?	117
33	What to read on Trump(ism)	123
	Bibliography	126
	Index	128

Acknowledgments

Chapter 1 is a revised version of the article "Definitions: Right, Far-Right, Outside Right and ... Just Trying To Be Populist," originally published in *HOPE not hate Magazine* (January–February 2016).
Chapter 3 was originally published in *Open Democracy* (23 September 2009).
Chapter 4 was originally published in *Open Democracy* (13 December 2012).
Chapter 5 was originally published in *Open Democracy* (3 September 2012).
Chapter 6 was originally published in *Open Democracy* (9 November 2012).
Chapter 7 was originally published in *Open Democracy* (28 October 2013).
Chapter 9 was originally published in the *Washington Post* (26 August 2015).
Chapter 10 was originally published in the *Huffington Post* (13 February 2016).
Chapter 11 was originally published in the *Huffington Post* (28 February 2016).
Chapter 12 was originally published in *HOPE not hate Magazine* (March–April 2016).
A shorter, and very different, version of Chapter 13 was published as "As American as Trump," in the *Boston Review* (13 June 2016).
Chapter 14 was originally published on the website *POP – Political Observer on Populism* (30 May 2016).
Chapter 15 was originally published in the *Huffington Post* (22 July 2016).
Chapter 16 was originally published in the *Huffington Post* (9 August 2016).
Chapter 17 was originally published in the *Huffington Post* (25 August 2016).

Chapter 18 was originally published in the *Huffington Post* (29 August 2016).

Chapter 19 was originally published in *HOPE not hate Magazine* (US Election Special, October 2016).

Chapter 20 was originally published in the *Huffington Post* (8 October 2016).

Chapter 21 was originally published in the *Huffington Post* (4 November 2016).

Chapter 22 was originally published in the *Huffington Post* (10 November 2016).

Chapter 23 was originally published as "Europe's Far Right Has Been Boosted By Trump's Win – For Now," in the *Guardian* (9 November 2016).

Chapter 24 was originally published in *Deutsche Welle* (29 November 2016).

Chapter 29 was originally published in *Newsweek* (15 December 2016).

Chapter 30 was originally published in *Newsweek* (30 December 2016).

Chapter 31 was originally published in the *Huffington Post* (20 March 2017).

Chapter 33 was originally published in the *Huffington Post* (23 September 2016).

Preface

I moved to the United States in September 2008, after having worked on far right movements and parties in Europe for some 15 years. In many ways, it was more a professional than a personal shock. Since I had started my PhD research on "the extreme right party family" at Leiden University, in 1993, "my" topic had become more and more relevant, by and large dominating academic and political debates on European politics in the 21st century. In the US, in sharp contrast, terms like "radical right" and "far right" featured sparsely in the political debate and generated little interest from scholars or students. That was 2008. How things have changed in ten years.

This spring I taught my course "Far Right Politics in Western Democracies" at the University of Georgia, as I have been doing almost every year since I came to the US. However, whereas students normally struggle to come up with a US example of the far right, usually only mentioning the Ku Klux Klan (KKK), now the specter of Donald Trump was hovering over our course throughout the semester. Like the rest of the country, my students were looking to Europe to better understand the US – a profoundly un-American attitude. To be fair, it was not easy to teach the course during such tumultuous times, in which people wanted to make sense of someone (Trump), and something (Trumpism), who in many ways wants to remain indefinable.

What the past year has shown us, at the very least, is that far right politics is not just a European phenomenon, or at best marginal within the US context. It is here, whether truly in power or "just" close to it. It also laid bare the lack of serious scholarship on the topic. There are more US-based political scientists who work on the far right in Europe than on the far right in the US! The situation in other disciplines is not much better. With the notable exception of some pioneers, like Kathleen Blee and Peter Simi, few sociologists study the US far right, and while historians have provided significant scholarship on US populism, most of it focuses exclusively on the original Populists of the People's Party, and their direct successors, more than 100 years ago. Indeed, much of the more significant work on the topic comes from activists and activist-scholars like Chip Berlet, Sara Diamond and Leonard Zeskind, or from non-Americans like Martin Durham.

This book does not intend to fill the many lacunas that exist in the scholarship of the far right in America. It is first and foremost aimed at a general audience in the hope to improve the political and public debate on the topic. However, it also aims to stimulate new scholarship on the topic by raising some questions on the historical antecedents, ideological features, and organizational weakness of "Trumpism," among others.

The Dutch historian Johan Huizinga, who was a great fan and scholar of America, once wrote that "it is the goal of the American university to be the brains of the republic." I would urge my colleagues, from a broad variety of disciplines, to break out of the increasingly narrow constraints of "real" academic research, and use "the brains of the republic" to adopt a broader disciplinary and regional approach to the study of American politics and society in general, and the far right in particular.

The past decades have seen the rise of various right-wing and far right movements, from the Christian Right in the 1980s to the Tea Party and Trump in the 21st century. All of them took US society by surprise, because journalists, practitioners and scholars did not look beyond the usual suspects of US politics. This has led to both over- and underestimation of the threat to American democracy. For example, on the one hand the rise of Donald Trump has been compared to that of Adolf Hitler in Weimar Germany, in line with the famous Godwin's Law, while on the other hand the issue of right-wing terrorism is barely addressed by academia, media, and politics.

While I have not directly consulted colleagues and friends when writing the various individual articles, which span a period of eight years, my understanding of US politics and society has been profoundly shaped by conversations and scholarship of many of them. Among my most important teachers of US politics in general, and the US far right in particular, are Chip Berlet, Clyde Wilcox, Dan Tichenor, Joe Lowndes, Kathleen Blee, Larry Rosenthal, Mark Potok, and Michael Kazin. Obviously, none of the errors and opinions are theirs, but I want to thank and recognize their insights and support in helping me navigate my new host country and its challenging politics and society.

Cas Mudde
Athens, GA, 11 May 2017

Abbreviations

AEI	American Enterprise Institute
AfD	Alternative for Germany
AIP	American Independence Party
ALEC	American Legislative Exchange Council
ANP	American Nazi Party
APSA	American Political Science Association
BNP	British National Party
CDA	Christian Democratic Appeal (The Netherlands)
CPAC	Conservative Political Action Conference
CSU	Christian Social Union (Germany)
DF	Danish People's Party
DHS	Department of Homeland Security
DUP	Democratic Unionist Party (Northern Ireland)
EDL	English Defence League
EU	European Union
FAIR	Federation for American Immigration Reform
FI	Forza Italia
FLNA	Fascist League of North America
FN	National Front (France)
FPÖ	Austrian Freedom Party
GOP	Grand Old Party
ISIS	Islamic State in Iraq and Syria
JBS	John Birch Society
KKK	Ku Klux Klan
NA	National Alliance
NATO	North Atlantic Treaty Organization
NPI	National Policy Institute
NSDAP	National Socialist German Workers' Party
NSM	National Socialist Movement
NSWPP	National Socialist White People's Party

PAC	political action committee
PEGIDA	Patriotic Europeans Against the Islamization of the West (Germany)
POP	Political Observer of Populism
PS	Socialist Party (France)
PVV	Party for Freedom (The Netherlands)
RaHoWa	racial holy war
RCT	Rational Choice Theory
RINO	Republican In Name Only
RNC	Republican National Committee
SGP	Politically Reformed Party (The Netherlands)
SPLC	Southern Poverty Law Center
SVP	Swiss People's Party
SYRIZA	Coalition of the Radical Left (Greece)
UK	United Kingdom
UKIP	UK Independence Party
UMP	Union for a Popular Movement (France)
UN	United Nations
US	United States
VVD	People's Party for Freedom and Democracy (The Netherlands)
WASP	White Anglo-Saxon Protestant

1 Definitions
The various shades of the US far right

This chapter presents a short discussion of the key terms associated with the topic of the book, most notably far right and radical right, and relates them both to each other and to their political context, i.e. (liberal) democracy.[1]

Regarding the far right, the general understanding seems to be that we know *who* they are even if we don't know exactly *what* they are. Even if this were to be true for each individual, it certainly doesn't hold at the general level. People disagree on what defines the far right, who its members are, and what term is best to use. Not surprisingly, these questions are related, even if many people are not necessarily aware of it.

What I will lay out here is *my* conceptual framework, i.e. an integrated collection of related but separate terms and definitions that are most often used with regard to the topic at hand, which I developed in more detail in my academic work.[2] It must be clear from the beginning that although there are several colleagues who roughly agree with this framework, many more do not. There is no consensus on terminology and there never will be.

The overarching term I use is *far right*, which encompasses both the extreme right and the radical right. The main difference between extremism and radicalism is the attitude towards democracy. Extremism fundamentally opposes democracy, here defined minimally as popular sovereignty and majority rule. In other words, extremists don't believe that the people should elect their leaders.

The *extreme right* comes in many shapes, from aristocrats to theocrats, but the most important subgroup is fascism. Fascism is fundamentally anti-democratic, believing in the *Führerprinzip* (leadership principle) instead. For fascists, all men are not created equal, not *between* nations/races, but also not *within*. Hitler and Mussolini were considered superior to other Germans and Italians and that is why they were destined to be their leaders, irrespective of majority rule. National Socialism (Nazism) is

2 Definitions: the shades of the US far right

often considered as a subtype of fascism, standing out for its centrality of anti-Semitism and racism.

It has become customary to use the terms fascism and Nazism only for the movements of the early 20th century and to add the prefix *neo* to similar movements in the postwar era. However, these groups are often only new in terms of their organization, and their members, being born after 1945. Ideologically they subscribe *grosso modo* to the old fascist/Nazi ideology. There are only a few groups that have really tried to modernize classic fascist ideologies, as such truly developing a neo-fascist ideology – the Italian group Casa Pound is a prime example. Most others, particularly the various so-called neo-Nazi groups, including the Greek party Golden Dawn (at least in its initial stage), are more accurately described as Nazi than neo-Nazi, especially in terms of their ideology.

The term *radical right* is best used for right-wing ideologies that accept democracy, i.e. popular sovereignty and majority rule, but oppose fundamental values of liberal democracy, notably minority rights and pluralism. The most relevant subgroup within the radical right is the *populist radical right*, which includes almost all relevant far right parties in contemporary Europe, including the Austrian Freedom Party (FPÖ), Danish People's Party (DF), the French National Front (FN), the Dutch Party for Freedom (PVV), and the Swiss People's Party (SVP). What all these parties have in common is a core ideology that combines nativism, authoritarianism, and populism.

Simply stated, nativism entails a combination of nationalism and xenophobia. It is an ideology that holds that states should be inhabited exclusively by members of the native group (the nation), and that non-native (or alien) elements, whether persons or ideas, are fundamentally threatening to the homogeneous nation-state. It is best summarized in the infamous slogan "Germany for the Germans, Foreigners Out!"

Authoritarianism refers to the belief in a strictly ordered society, in which infringements of authority are to be punished severely. This translates into strict law and order policies, which call for more police with greater competencies and less political involvement in the judiciary. Often crime and immigration are directly connected; such as, for example, in the PVV slogan "more safety, less immigration," or the infamous racist SVP poster in which a white sheep kicks a black sheep out of Switzerland under the slogan "creating security."

Populism, finally, is an ideology that considers society to be ultimately separated into two homogeneous and antagonistic groups, the pure people and the corrupt elite, and which argues that politics should be an expression of the *volonté générale* (general will) of the people. Populist radical right politicians claim to be *vox populi* (the voice of the people), and accuse the established parties of being in cahoots with each other – as aptly captured in the FN's reference to "UMPS," a combination of the abbreviations of the party names of the center-right Union for a Popular Movement (UMP) and center-left Socialist Party (PS).

This still leaves one key term to be defined: *right*. Although the distinction between left and right is essential to virtually any discussion about politics, both terms are used in various ways and their meaning has changed drastically in the past centuries. Initially referring to supporters (left) and opponents (right) of the French Revolution, the terms became more linked to secular versus religious in the 19th century, and state versus market in the 20th century. Today the socio-economic dimension is still predominant, but it is increasingly combined with a socio-cultural dimension relating to an ever-growing range of attitudes and issues – including European integration and immigration.

Most of these dimensions are captured in the definition of the Italian philosopher Norberto Bobbio,[3] who sees the key distinction between left and right in the view on (in)equality: the *left* considers the key inequalities between people to be artificial and negative, which should be overcome by an active state; whereas the *right* believes that the main inequalities between people are natural and positive, to be defended by the state.

Within the US context, groups like the National Socialist Movement (NSM) and the so-called "alt-right" (see Chapter 17) represent the extreme right, while Breitbart News and paleoconservatives like Patrick (Pat) Buchanan represent the radical right. Because of the dominance of the two-party system, the two main political parties have never been pure examples of far right politics, even though both have (had) at times significant radical right factions – such as the so-called Dixiecrats, i.e. the Southern faction of the Democratic Party until the 1970s, or several of the Republican Party's Tea Party Caucus members in Congress more recently. Whether Donald Trump is transforming the Republican Party into a true radical right party will be at the center of many of the chapters in this book.

Notes

1 This chapter is a revised version of the article "Definitions: Right, Far-Right, Outside Right and … Just Trying To Be Populist," originally published in *HOPE not hate Magazine* (January–February 2016).
2 See, most notably, chapters 1 and 2 of my *Populist Radical Right Parties in Europe* (New York: Cambridge University Press, 2007).
3 See Norberto Bobbio, *Left and Right: The Significance of a Political Distinction* (Chicago, IL: University of Chicago Press, 1997).

2 A short history of the far right in America

Although far right politics is more generally associated with Europe rather than America, the US has a long history of far right politics, dating back, at the very least, to the Know Nothings of the mid-19th century. This chapter chronicles some of the main US far right groups of the past 150 years.

Before the election of Donald Trump to the presidency, the radical right was mostly associated with Europe in US media. For most Americans, far right politics was something on the margins of US politics with, at best, some troublesome history during the era of the struggle for civil rights in the South in the 1960s. In that sense, their knowledge of the US radical right went barely beyond the movie *Mississippi Burning*. Even though the rise of Trump has changed these dynamics, most of my students will still consider far right politics to be established in European history, yet exceptional in US history.

They are surprised to hear that, in fact, far right politics has a much longer history in America than in Europe, particularly as a political force. Nativism has been a powerful electoral force in the US at least since the mid-19th century. However, the far right has mostly failed to establish itself as a federal force, because of a lack of organization and the strength of the two-party system. Still, at least at the state and local levels far right forces have been highly influential during various (longer and shorter) "episodes." And in much of the (Deep) South far right forces were only really marginalized in the 1980s.

2.1 The Know Nothings

Ironically, the contemporary anti-immigration parties in Europe can, in many ways, be seen as a modern version of the infamous Native American Party, later renamed the American Party, of the mid-19th century. Better known as the Know Nothing movement – because members of the secretive organization were expected to answer to questions about its activities with "I know nothing" – the American Party was probably the first purely nativist party of the Western world. And it was far from marginal! Railing against Catholic immigrants from Ireland and Germany, the American Party gained significant political power at the local and regional levels. At its peak, it had 52 members in the House of Representatives (1854) and five senators (1856). Know Nothings were also responsible for serious public violence, particularly around mayoral elections in cities like Baltimore and Louisville. But, as is typical in US history, the American Party disappeared as quickly as it had emerged, being back to zero members of Congress in 1860.

2.2 The second coming of the Klan

Although no major nativist organization emerged until the second coming of the Ku Klux Klan in the 1920s, the period between 1860 and 1920 saw many nativist pieces of legislation and riots, directed against a broad range of "others," from primarily the Chinese on the West Coast to predominantly the Catholic Germans on the East Coast. Originally founded by defeated Confederate soldiers, in the wake of the Civil War, the KKK re-emerged with a vengeance in the 1920s – in part sparked by the cinematographically beautiful, but historically inaccurate, movie *Birth of a Nation* (1915), which romanticized the first Klan as heroic protectors of embattled whites in the South.

The Second Klan was a much bigger movement, extending well beyond the South, creating strongholds in the Midwest, with an alleged 80,000 Klansmen in Detroit alone. The Second Klan still defended WASP (White Anglo-Saxon Protestant) society but its enemies were no longer just African Americans, but also, and in some areas primarily, Catholic European immigrants and Jews. Estimates vary wildly, but some of the highest put the total membership of the KKK at 4 million in the 1920s, which would have constituted some 15 percent of the US population at that time. While the Klan was never able to establish a solid organization at the federal level, Klansmen held high-ranking political positions at all levels throughout the country, including in US Congress. The organization started to decrease sharply after the Great Depression, falling back to a mere 30,000 members nationwide in 1930.

2.3 The fascist era

While the US had many fascist organizations during the interwar period, most of the larger groups were linked to specific European immigrant groups. Among the most popular were the pro-Nazi German American Bund, which had some 25,000 members at its peak, and the much smaller Italian-American Fascist League of North America (FLNA). In addition, some prominent Americans more or less openly supported European fascism, including Charles Edward "Father" Coughlin, who had a very popular radio show, and aviator Charles A. Lindbergh, prominent spokesman of the America First Committee, which was primarily against US involvement in the Second World War but also harbored many US admirers of European fascism.

After the defeat of Nazi Germany the US would still be home to myriad Nazi and neo-Nazi groups, thanks to its broad interpretation of freedom of speech. The most notable was the American Nazi Party (ANP), founded by George Lincoln Rockwell in 1959, and later renamed as the National Socialist White People's Party (NSWPP) – in case people didn't get the link to Adolf Hitler's National Socialist German Workers' Party (NSDAP). Although the party continues to exist, it was always marginal, with no notable electoral activity, mainly living off media attention. The same applies for groups like the National Alliance (NA) and the National Socialist Movement (NSM), which are more like cults or gangs than political parties.

2.4 The civil rights era

Radical right sentiments played a noticeable role in the anti-communist movement of the 1950s and 1960s, and particularly in prominent organizations like the John Birch Society (JBS), but the movement itself cannot be categorized as radical right. Moreover, the movement organized mostly within the existing political parties, the Republican Party in particular. At the same time, radical right sentiments in the South mobilized within the Democratic Party. The so-called Dixiecrats combined support for segregation and welfare chauvinism, targeting primarily African Americans in the Jim Crow South.

When the civil rights movement became a threat to "Southern life," the KKK made its second return, again mainly as a Southern phenomenon. Its power was mostly local, where Klan members and sympathizers would dominate towns' police and politics, although many Southern states had senators with Klan ties. Moreover, Klan members were responsible for an orgy of violence in the South, and beyond, often helped by activists of other extreme right groups – such as the Greensboro massacre of 1979, in which five protesters from the Communist Workers' Party were shot and killed by KKK and American Nazi Party members.

Alabama Governor George Wallace became the voice of the Southern pro-segregation movement, mounting the most significant challenge to the two-party system in recent history. After running unsuccessfully in the 1964 Democratic primaries, he challenged the two-party system as a third-party candidate for the American Independence Party (AIP), winning a stunning 13.5 percent of the votes in the 1968 presidential election. Moreover, Wallace won five Southern states (Alabama, Arkansas, Georgia, Louisiana, and Mississippi) – even right-wing populist Ross Perot, who won a record 18.9 percent as the third-party candidate for the Reform Party in 1992, was unable to win even one state. It would be the last big stand of the Southern far right, although smaller KKK and neo-Confederate groups remain disproportionately active in the region.

2.5 The late 20th century

As the traditional far right of the KKK entered the same marginal space of US politics as neo-Nazi groups and parties, increasingly overlapping in members and organizations, radical right politics became more and more linked to anti-immigration politics and to anti-government positions – sometimes, but not always, combined. Most of the anti-immigration politics was initiated by non-party groups, like the Federation for American Immigration Reform (FAIR) and NumbersUSA of John Tanton, which worked through sympathetic Republican lawmakers at the local, state, and federal levels (such as Senators Steve King of Iowa and Jeff Sessions of Alabama). FAIR lawyer Kris Kobach was the mastermind behind the phrase "self-deportation," which haunted Mitt Romney during the 2012 presidential election.

While the anti-immigration movement is well funded and organized, and operates at the federal level too, the anti-government movement is mostly grassroots, limited to the local and state levels. Anti-government extremism has a long history in the US, but became particularly forceful in the 1990s, in the so-called militia movement. Linked to issues like the Second Amendment and state rights, militias proliferated in the 1990s, mostly in the West and Midwest, influencing local conservative and Republican groups and members. Their rise was cut short by the Oklahoma City bombing of 1995, committed by Timothy McVeigh, who had been part of the broader militia movement. The US government came down hard on the movement and the number of groups decreased rapidly. However, they would make a strong comeback under President Barack Obama, with the Southern Poverty Law Center (SPLC) counting a staggering 1,360 "patriot" groups in 2012.

8 *A short history of the far right in America*

While this is only a very partial summary of some of the main far right groups of the past roughly 150 years of US history, it shows that far right parties are neither new nor really marginal in America. They have always been around, although generally more as grassroots groups and movements at the local and state levels, rather than nationally organized political parties. The following chapters will focus explicitly on the US far right in the 21st century, which, in one way or another, is rooted in this long and varied history.

3 The Tea Party paradox

The Tea Party movement holds the US Constitution in high regard and claims to defend the original intentions of the Founding Fathers. Ironically, like many other right-wing actors, they get entangled in the fundamental distinction between the Jeffersonian and Madisonian traditions of US politics.[1]

Anyone familiar with the basics of American history knows that the Constitution was the outcome of time-pressured compromises between various political camps, notably the Federalists and the Anti-Federalists. One of the key points that every "Introduction to American Government" textbook stresses is the struggle between two very different ways of looking at democracy, and the role of the people therein, each linked to a prominent Founding Father.[2]

On the one hand, we have the elitist view of democracy associated with America's fourth president, James Madison. He saw the people as naturally self-interested and wanted therefore to limit their participation in government, arguing that too much democracy was a bad thing. On the other hand, we have the populist view of democracy espoused by Thomas Jefferson, the third president of the United States. Jefferson saw the people as inherently virtuous and believed that individuals act not just for their own good, but for the common good. There is no doubt that Jefferson won the fight over the preamble, but lost the battle over the Constitution. Many crucial elements of the Constitution reflected Madison's distrust of the people and his preference for limited democracy. In fact, the institutions of the federal government were intentionally designed to insulate them from the desires of the people (e.g. no direct elections except for the House of Representatives), not to make them beholden and reflexive to the masses.

The distinction between Madisonian and Jeffersonian views of democracy are not purely historical, however. Paradoxically, while Madison won the battle over the Constitution, the most important document of American politics, Jefferson has left a lasting legacy in American culture, helped by the preamble's powerful opening reference to "We the People," in shaping the dominant discourse of American politics. Politicians of both the Democratic Party and Republican Party will invoke "the people" as the almighty sovereign and argue that democracy is government "of the people, by the people, for the people," as President Abraham Lincoln famously declared. And no politician will dare to defend an elitist interpretation of democracy. Essential to a successful campaign is for a politician to identify her- or himself with "the people" and to distinguish her- or himself from "the elite" (even clear elites like Al Gore and George W. Bush tried to do this).

Today, the loudest voice of "the people" and the Jeffersonian view of democracy is the Tea Party. Conservative Sam Tanenhaus recently stated that Jefferson "has had many ideological successors, up through today's Tea Party movement" (*New York Times*, 30 July 2011). Indeed, you cannot go to a Tea Party demonstration or meeting without seeing "We the People" signs or hearing speeches and slogans about the need for the people to take back the government.

The irony is that today's loudest supporters of Jeffersonian democracy are also the staunchest defenders of the Madisonian Constitution. Somehow, they fail to understand that a rigid originalist interpretation of the Constitution only strengthens the elitist system of limited democracy at the expense of "We the People."

Notes

1 This chapter was first published in *Open Democracy* (23 September 2009).
2 For an accessible and very thought-provoking book on the US Constitution, as well as its Framers (Founders), see Robert Dahl, *How Democratic is the American Constitution?* (New Haven, CT: Yale University Press, 2003, 2nd edition).

4 Wisconsin's Sikh massacre
The real danger

The perpetrator of the latest mass shooting in the United States has been compared to Timothy McVeigh and Anders Breivik. But a closer understanding of his motives and actions is needed before making this connection.[1]

The United States has in the past month experienced two mass shootings. The first was on July 20, 2012, at a midnight film screening in a cinema in Aurora, Colorado, when twelve people were killed and seventy injured; the second was on August 5, at a Sikh temple in Oak Tree, Wisconsin, where six were killed and three injured.

In both cases the perpetrator was a single white male, aged 24 and 40 respectively (the Aurora gunman, James Eagan Holmes, was detained, while the Oak Tree one, Wade Michael Page, was shot by the police before killing himself). Beyond these similarities, however, the treatment of the Wisconsin murders in the media is distinguished by a focus on its alleged political motive: namely, white supremacy.

The fact that the killer in Wisconsin embraced a xenophobic ideology has led commentators to compare the shooting at the Sikh temple not so much to the Colorado incident but rather to two earlier "extreme right terrorist acts": the bombing of a federal building in Oklahoma City by Timothy McVeigh in 1995, and the Oslo bombing and Utøya massacre by Anders Breivik in 2011. But although this and other similarities should be taken into account, so should the differences, which are at least as important.

4.1 The background

It is necessary to bear in mind that, at the time of writing, it is still not known exactly why Page went on his shooting-spree and why he chose the unlikely target of a Sikh temple. The post-9/11 experience, when there were many examples of Sikhs in the US being attacked and targeted because they were wrongly identified as Muslims, has led analysts to assume that Page was in the grip of the same "mistake." There are two reasons why this seems unconvincing.

First, members of the white supremacist movement, though normally not the best-educated members of society, do tend to know their enemies. So, for example, after Wisconsin several white supremacists in the US commented on blogs and websites (such as Stormfront) that Sikhs were among the "least threatening" of non-white immigrant groups. In the United Kingdom, the British National Party (BNP) has even explicitly reached out to British Sikhs, whom they see as both the most pro-British and the most Islamophobic of the immigrant communities; while the radical right activist group the English Defence League (EDL) counts a Sikh (Guramit Singh) among its members, and has created an opportunistic anti-Muslim alliance with some local Sikhs in the town of Luton, north of London.

Second, the city of Milwaukee – of which Oak Tree is a suburb – has a fairly sizeable Muslim community, with one of its mosques, the Masjid al-Huda, only six miles from the Sikh temple. It's true that Page had only recently moved to Milwaukee, but if Islamophobia was his main motive, it remains to be explained why he wasn't able to identify an actual Muslim target within his reach.

This leads to the two main differences between Page, on the one hand, and McVeigh and Breivik, on the other. First, the level of planning. McVeigh had prepared his attack for months, and in some level of cooperation with others (he had to rent a truck, collect explosives, and so on). Breivik too had spent months organizing his operation, from stashing guns to wiping clean his hard-drive. By contrast, Page arrived at the temple with just one handgun, legally purchased about a month earlier (which makes him possibly the least-armed mass shooter in modern American history). This probably also explains why, fortunately, the human toll of his attacks was much lower than that of Breivik or the Aurora shooter.

Second, the ideological background. Both McVeigh and Breivik were connected to radical ideologies and subcultures that were well connected to mainstream discourse. McVeigh was a classic product of the paranoid militia subculture of the 1990s (which has actually made a strong resurgence, albeit in a different guise, during Barack Obama's presidency). Breivik took his inspiration from radical right politicians such as Geert Wilders, but also from American conservatives such as Bruce Bawer and Daniel Pipes. Hence, while his actions were universally condemned, some accounts of the tragedy referred to his motives in approving terms.

Page, in sharp contrast, roamed in the dark depths of white power music, a scene so obscure and marginal that it took journalists a couple of days to produce even a rudimentary portrait. The broader white power and neo-Nazi currents are completely beyond the pale of even far right politics in the United States, and the main watchdog body describes their former leading organization, the National Alliance, as a "joke."

4.2 The consequences

The implication of these factors is that the US authorities should direct their attention less to "hatecore," to possible international connections and extreme right terrorism, and more to the threat of extreme right individuals in general, and former military with extreme right ideas in particular. This was done in the wake of the Oklahoma City bombing, although the (ex-)military connection was quickly sidetracked; moreover, because of recruiting problems for its wars in Afghanistan and Iraq, the US military relaxed its no-extremism policy for several years.

In 2009, the incoming Obama administration published a report by the Department of Homeland Security (DHS), entitled *Rightwing Extremism: Current Economic and Political Climate Fueling Resurgence in Radicalization and Recruitment*.[2] It warned explicitly of potential violence from former military personnel with extreme right ideas. The right-wing media and political elite were furious, even accusing Obama and the DHS Secretary, Janet Napolitano, of a "hit job on conservatives." The administration withdrew its report and, it seems, reassigned most of its researchers to supposedly more important threats. The leading desk analyst, Daryl Johnson, tried to refocus attention to the threat of the extreme right, but his failure to convince his colleagues led him to resign.

The fruits of this neglect may well have become apparent in the Wisconsin incident. This makes it essential that the Obama administration addresses the danger of violence from the extreme right with new seriousness. The various preventative actions by law enforcement agencies make clear that the extreme right is being watched. But it is even more vital that the administration is more explicit and open about what it perceives as the main threats.

Clearly, this should not become a witch-hunt, either of people with extreme right ideas or of (former) military personnel. But the combination of extremist ideas (of whatever political or religious persuasion) and military experience is potentially deadly – as Oklahoma City, the Fort Hood shooting in 2009, and now Oak Tree show. Citizens deserve a watchful state, but also an open state, which can be held accountable for its surveillance. As a first step, the Obama administration should reinstate the 2009 report and reassign a significant number of analysts to the DHS' extreme right desk.

Notes

1 This chapter was first published in *Open Democracy* (13 December 2012).
2 The report can be downloaded for free at: https://fas.org/irp/eprint/rightwing.pdf.

5 America's new revolutionaries

The belief that the United States stands at a historic crossroads is widespread across the political spectrum. But among parts of the right the view takes worrying directions.[1]

In the past few weeks a lot of publicity has been given to "RaHoWa," the fictional "Racial Holy War" proclaimed by white supremacists, mostly in songs and on internet forums such as Stormfront. This relatively obscure and murky world was brought into the media spotlight after the horrific shooting on August 5, 2012, in a Sikh temple in Wisconsin by Wade Michael Page (see Chapter 4). While he never gave an explanation for his deeds, and took his own life during the shooting, it has become received wisdom that this was his contribution to RaHoWa.

The Wisconsin tragedy has refocused attention on the right-wing fringe in America, in particular the white supremacist and sovereign citizen movements. This is important, if only because of the previous obsessive focus on Islamic terrorism at the expense of every other terrorist threat; but it is not where the main battle call for the "new American revolution" is coming from. Much more worryingly, revolutionary discourse – including calls for "armed resistance" to an alleged totalitarian state – is coming from the mainstream of American society, uncritically amplified by some major media outlets.

Since the inauguration of Barack Obama, America's first non-white president, the Southern Poverty Law Center (SPLC) has noted a staggering increase in right-wing mobilization. In fact, the number of groups, including mostly so-called "patriot" and "sovereign citizens" groups, has now surpassed that of the 1990s, the height of the militia movement (which imploded in the wake of the Oklahoma City bombing of 1995). Yet while this trend is unsettling in itself, and requires more debate and state supervision, a much more worrying development has taken place in the mainstream, rather than the fringes, of American society: the radicalization of the angry white man.

16 *America's new revolutionaries*

Many commentators have noted the "anger" within the Tea Party movement as well as the conspiracy theories that abound within it. The idea that Barack Obama is a secret Muslim socialist hell-bent on destroying "the America of our forefathers" is a sentiment not restricted to the odd ones out. Most rallies I have attended saw various people with signs relating to this conspiracy theory and were generally met with open approval rather than condemnation by the broader crowd. But while it is certainly disturbing that more than half of Republican Party voters think that Obama was not born in the US and that 34 percent of conservative Republicans think he is a Muslim, in and by themselves these opinions don't have to lead to anything more than "loyal opposition".

5.1 The toxic take-back

A much more alarming trend within the right-wing movement, of which the (amorphous) Tea Party is just the loudest and most prominent representative, is the growth of outright "disloyal" opposition, in which the whole state becomes the enemy. One of the crudest examples, though itself one among many, came from Tom Head, a judge in Lubbock County, Texas. Combining the now dominant frame that the upcoming presidential election is the most important in the country's history, the last chance to, in Romney's terms, "take America back" (from what – the Muslims, the socialists?), and long-standing right-wing fears of a United Nations (UN) invasion, Head told the local Fox affiliate Fox34 News:

> He's going to try to hand over the sovereignty of the United States to the UN, and what is going to happen when that happens? I'm thinking the worst. Civil unrest, civil disobedience, civil war maybe. And we're not just talking a few riots here and demonstrations, we're talking Lexington, Concord, take up arms and get rid of the guy. Now what's going to happen if we do that, if the public decides to do that? He's going to send in UN troops. I don't want 'em in Lubbock County. OK. So I'm going to stand in front of their armored personnel carrier and say "you're not coming in here." And the sheriff, I've already asked him, I said "you gonna back me" he said, "yeah, I'll back you." Well, I don't want a bunch of rookies back there. I want trained, equipped, seasoned veteran officers to back me.[2]

As shocking as this statement might be to many, it touches upon sentiments broadly shared within the American right-wing. In fact, I was probably even more struck by the Fox34 News response to the rant: "Whether you agree with the judge, or think his theories are unrealistic, the reality is a tax hike that will provide an additional $832,433 coupled with $2 million in cuts to make the numbers work." Clearly they were not bothered by this thinly veiled threat of armed resistance to legitimate state power.

5.2 The twin target

The belief that America is at a historic crossroads, and that the 2012 election could be the last one, is widespread within America's right-wing circles. That's expressed in the slogan "Defend America. Defeat Obama," popular on t-shirts and bumper stickers, or in organizations like the Save America Foundation. But while the ideas might be expressed more radically on the fringes of the right-wing movement, they have become well-established within the right-wing establishment too.

For example, Tom Sowell writes about "The Un-American Vision of Barack Obama" in the *National Review Online* (22 August 2012), based on the popular book *The Roots of Obama's Rage* (2010), authored by radical right entrepreneur Dinish D'Souza, while Larry Klayman – on the popular conservative WorldNetDaily (WND) website – calls Obama a traitor, "sympathetic not to Judeo-Christians values and culture, but Islam and its surrogate-controlled states."

Anti-governmental attitudes are, of course, nothing new within the American right. Unlike in Europe, where the right traditionally has been close to the state and has at times heralded the state as the prime loyalty of each citizen (even higher than God), political culture in the United States has always been less statist, on both the left and the right. Still, it is a far cry from Ronald Reagan's mantra, "government is not the solution to our problem, government is the problem," to the contemporary right-wing's demand to "take America back." While most mainstream Republicans do not call for armed resistance, their message of doom and increasing use of conspiracy theories seems to leave no other viable option (particularly if Obama wins re-election).

The last years of right-wing propaganda have led to a process that the late Israeli terrorism expert Ehud Sprinzak terms "split delegitimization," a trajectory through which the right-wing comes to terrorism.[3] Traditionally the right-wing will have its primary conflict with an "inferior" community, mostly (ethnic, political, or religious) minorities, and consider the state as an ally, sympathetic to its cause. Once it feels that the state is captured by the "inferior" enemy (i.e. the Muslim socialist Barack Hussein Obama), it will enter into a secondary conflict with the government. It is here that more or less unorganized political violence, like Page in Wisconsin, is transformed into more or less organized terrorism, such as McVeigh in Oklahoma City.

5.3 The real threat

All this does not imply that the average right-wing American is a terrorist-in-waiting, or that the Tea Party is a terrorist organization. Most such people will abhor violence in general, and violence against fellow Americans in particular. But it does mean that the extremist rhetoric that comes from so-called law-abiding patriots should be taken more seriously. Over the past two decades most acts of political violence in the United States have come from the right, even if the attacks of Muslim extremists were deadlier. Between the highly destructive Oklahoma City bombing of April 1995 and 9/11 – the deadliest terrorist attack on American soil – there were more than fifty (planned) acts of right-wing violence.[4] In many cases the target represented the government/state, including law enforcement agents.

In this light, it is particularly interesting to see how lax law enforcement agencies have dealt with these thinly veiled threats of violence compared to their heavy-handed approach to the alleged threat from radical Muslims and radical left activists (including animal rights activists and environmentalists). Most responsibility lies with the right-wing establishment, however. Republican Party leaders should be more careful in choosing their company and insinuations.

They should also stop their obstruction of state investigations of right-wing threats, such as the concerted effort to kill the Department of Homeland Security's 2009 report, entitled *Rightwing Extremism: Current Economic and Political Climate Fueling Resurgence in Radicalization and Recruitment* (see Chapter 4). After all, if they really love their country and its "heroes" (which includes law enforcement agents), they should protect these objects of their concern.

Notes

1 This chapter was first published in *Open Democracy* (3 September 2012).
2 See "Texas Judge Warns of 'Civil Unrest,' UN Troop Presence if Obama Re-Elected," *Fox News*, 23 August 2012.
3 See Ehud Sprinzak, "Right-Wing Terrorism in a Comparative Perspective: The Case of Split Delegitimization," *Terrorism and Political Violence*, Vol. 7, No. 1, 1995, pp.17–43.
4 For an overview, see SPLC, "Terror of the Right," 1 November 2015, available at: www.splcenter.org/20100126/terror-right (last visited on 1 May 2017).

6 America's election and the Tea Party

A series of voting setbacks in November 2012 means the conservative Tea Party movement is now facing a difficult and divisive period. The ball is now in President Obama's corner.[1]

What a difference two years make. After the congressional elections in November 2010, the Tea Party was the talk of the town. Both left-wing and right-wing media pundits declared "the" Tea Party to be the (only) winner, and all focus was on the right's new stars such as Rand Paul in Kentucky and Marco Rubio in Florida. The new Republican Party kingmakers were Jim DeMint and Sarah Palin, support from whom was claimed to be essential for their fellow Republicans to get elected. It became obligatory to refer to the new legislature as "the Tea Party Congress." The fact that only one-third of Tea Party-backed candidates had actually been elected was irrelevant. The Tea Party was the new story, and all experts knew that it was here to stay.

An aptly titled Fox News story – "After election victories, Tea Party activists look ahead to 2012" (5 November 2010) – speculated about the movement's future. It seemed beyond debate that it was the newly dominant force in US politics; the question was whether it was going to take over the Republican Party or create a third party. Within a month of the November 2010 elections the answer to that question became clear: helped by massive spending by "AstroTurf" organizations such as FreedomWorks, and led by members of the Grand Old Party (GOP) establishment, the Tea Party was steadily integrated into the GOP. But who controlled whom?

Even before the Republican primaries started for the 2012 elections, the media were unified in their narrative: the Tea Party was going to select the GOP's presidential nominee. This narrative was strengthened by the strong, if in the end brief, showings of Tea Party favorites like Minnesota's Michelle Bachmann and former pizza CEO Herman Cain. Bachmann even gave the first-ever official Tea Party response to President Obama's

State of the Union address in 2011, which was broadcast live on national television by CNN! In the end, however, no Tea Party candidate could really challenge the old-school Republican-establishment candidate, Mitt Romney. The Tea Party's influence on the primaries remained limited to pushing Romney to make very right-wing promises on issues like immigration, which would haunt him during the actual campaign.

6.1 From defeat ...

At the height of the election campaign, the Tea Party was almost invisible. The campaign was dominated by the (Super) PACs (political action committees) of Mitt Romney and GOP establishment operatives like Karl Rove, who together spent the astounding amount of over $310 million. Even Romney's choice of running-mate, Ayn Rand devotee Paul Ryan, was more the darling of the AstroTurf Tea Party boosters in Wall Street than of the grassroots Tea Party activists in Main Street. Moreover, Ryan ("Mr Budget") had to defend Romney's much more moderate agenda on both fiscal and social issues. In fact, in almost every scandal involving a Republican candidate for Congress, which mostly related to outlandish remarks on abortion or rape (often positions that Ryan had supported in his pre-vice president nominee period), Romney joined the condemnations from the Republican establishment, albeit it at times halfheartedly – even when the offending candidates were Tea Party favorites such as Senate hopefuls Todd Akin from Missouri and Richard Mourdock from Indiana.

In the end, and in virtually all ways, the 2012 elections were a total defeat for the Tea Party – a rare exception was the election to the Senate of Ted Cruz in Texas. The movement was not just unable to oust President Obama, its number-one priority, but saw some of its most prominent candidates fail in the congressional votes. Both Todd ("legitimate rape") Akin and Richard ("pregnancy resulting from rape is God's will") Mourdock paid the price for their extreme statements. In Akin's case this meant that the GOP lost out on a sure pick-up seat, while Mourdock was responsible for taking the Senate seat from Richard Lugar, the longstanding and well-respected Republican senator, and handing it to the Democrats.

Even Tea Party incumbents fared very badly. Scott Brown, the Massachusetts senator, for a while the very personification of the Tea Party's power, was handsomely defeated by Elizabeth Warren, the new hope of the American left. Two leaders of the Tea Party caucus in Congress, Florida's Allen "progressives are communists" West and

Illinois's "Crazy" Joe Walsh, lost their seats in the House of Representatives (West called for a recount). On top of that, Michelle "the Founders worked tirelessly against slavery" Bachmann was only re-elected by the narrowest of margins after outspending her opponent twelve-to-one. In short, the Tea Party failed miserably, and the GOP establishment has taken notice.

6.2 ... to division

What, then, do the 2012 elections reveal about the Tea Party's future? If anything, the elections show that extreme social-conservative statements are not appreciated by most Americans – even among many religious and Republican voters. While AstroTurf Tea Party operatives claim that the Tea Party has recently been "hijacked" by social conservatives, academic research notes the crucial importance of anti-abortion and anti-immigration positions to grassroots Tea Party supporters.[2] In short, there is no Tea Party without (extreme) social conservatism, but there is no GOP national majority with (extreme) social conservatism.

The leaders of both factions threw their first punches on the night of the presidential count. Republican establishment leaders said that Mitt Romney had lost because the Tea Party had pushed him too far to the right in the primaries, while Tea Party leaders argued that he had not gone far enough to the right. The struggle for dominance of the GOP was on. The veteran conservative operative and prominent Tea Party figure Richard A. Vigueri boasted: "Tea Partiers will take over the Republican Party within four years."

The Republican elite seems convinced that the only way to survive as a viable alternative to the Democratic Party is to become less radical and more inclusive. Among the most vocal protagonists of a more diverse party strategy is former Tea Party favorite Marco Rubio; the Cuban-American senator from Florida is calling for the GOP to abandon its "white strategy" and embrace America's Hispanics, the key demographic in many (southern) Democratic states. A more ethnically diverse Republican strategy will have to include some level of support for comprehensive immigration reform, which will antagonize a Tea Party strongly nativist at local level.

It is a paradox, though, that immigration is for the Tea Party movement both a strength and a weakness – even if not all Tea Partiers consider immigration a high priority. If and when President Obama finally makes good on his word to enact comprehensive immigration reform, the Tea Party movement will split. The AstroTurf faction is mostly bankrolled by big business, which favors liberal immigration policies, while the grassroots faction is largely anti-immigration. Without financial support from the AstroTurf groups, and sympathetic media coverage from major outlets like Fox News, the Tea Party will be returned to its true proportions: i.e. a relatively strong local and regional force in some parts of the country, but a relatively weak force in national politics. So, the initiative is with the re-elected president.

Notes

1 This chapter was first published in *Open Democracy* (9 November 2012).
2 See, for instance, Theda Skocpol and Vanessa Williamson, *The Tea Party and the Remaking of Republican Conservatism* (New York: Oxford University Press, 2011).

7 Is the revolution eating its children?
The Tea Party between AstroTurf and grassroots

The 2014 GOP primaries will show whether the Tea Party was indeed just an AstroTurf invention, as many liberals have claimed, or a true grassroots movement, as most conservatives proclaim.[1]

The past weeks have seen the return of the Tea Party to center stage of American politics. The movement that took the country by storm in 2009, dominated (the media coverage of) the 2010 election, but largely failed in the 2012 election (see Chapter 6), was now responsible for a government shutdown and almost caused the country's default. Thousands of articles and op-eds were written about the extremism and irresponsibility of the "Tea Party Congress" and about the spinelessness and weakness of the "moderate" Republicans.

What a difference a day makes. While the Tea Party was controlling the GOP after the government shutdown, that same Tea Party is the big loser of the failed attempt to block the raising of the debt ceiling. Pointing to a "dramatic decrease" in public support, the Tea Party is again predicted to "die" in the near future. After all, the shutdown has led to a "widened GOP-Tea Party rift" and has angered the big financial backers of the party. *Bloomberg* (18 October 2013) even predicts a "Republican Civil War" of "Business Groups v. Tea Party." Out of nowhere (mainstream right-wing) pundits come out of hiding and offer advice on how the Republicans can "neutralize" the Tea Party. There is again money in being an anti-Tea Party Republican!

The last couple of weeks are also very exciting from an academic perspective. From its first emergence pundits and scholars have been divided over the question of whether the Tea Party is mainly an AstroTurf, i.e. big business and professional (Republican) operatives like FreedomWorks, or mainly a grassroots phenomenon, like the Tea Party Patriots, a loose federation of local and regional Tea Party groups. Where the two factions are united in their rejection of Obama (care), and "thus" the government shutdown, they are bitterly divided over the debt ceiling. Unsurprisingly, the AstroTurf faction won the fight in Congress. No sooner had the influential Koch brothers spoken out against a national default, and House Speaker John Boehner started to lay the discursive foundations for a deal on raising the debt ceiling. But as soon as the Republicans had enabled the raising of the debt ceiling grassroots Tea Partiers opened the attack, among others on the Facebook page of Speaker Boehner.

The fact that the (mostly non-Tea Party) Republicans in Congress caved and changed their position on the debt ceiling is in no way evidence that the Tea Party is a pure AstroTurf phenomenon. It mainly shows that professional politicians are more susceptible to money than people; hardly news. Moreover, most Tea Party Republicans opposed the compromise, despite the "advice" from big business. One of the reasons is that conservative Republicans have been able to fundraise more independently from the party leadership. Central to this strategy is Tea Party favorite Jim DeMint, the former senator of South Carolina who left to lead the Heritage Foundation, which through the new Heritage Action tries to provide financial independence for the conservative/Tea Party GOP candidates. While the Heritage Foundation sided with big business on the compromise over the debt ceiling, DeMint was quick to praise the "courageous leadership" of Senators Ted Cruz (R-Texas) and Mike Lee (R-Utah) and proclaim his unwavering opposition to Obamacare.

Equally important is that many surveys show remarkable support for the Tea Party and its extreme positions. While liberals, and (secretly) "moderate" Republicans, celebrate that "nearly half (49 percent) of the public now view the Tea Party unfavorably," they forget that the 30 percent who view it favorably constitute the vast majority of the (open) Republicans. Moreover, while Republicans' views of "moderate" GOP leaders have become less positive, those of Tea Party senators like Ted Cruz have remained stable for all Republicans and have become significantly more positive for Tea Party Republicans. Moreover, various academic studies have shown the increasing overlap between Tea Party supporters and GOP supporters as well as their values.[2] Tea Party values are not fundamentally different from GOP values. In essence, Tea Partiers are mostly more extreme and negative, which is a direct consequence of the low trust in the political system of Tea Party supporters.

So, where does that leave the Tea Party? Is the (Tea) Party over? I seriously doubt it is. This seems mostly wishful thinking of liberals and "moderate" Republicans. And they have been wrong many times before. The Tea Party has always been AstroTurf *and* grassroots, united in their fight against a vaguely defined enemy, Obama(care), and divided on both the means and the ends of their struggle. In many ways, it is the anti-globalization movement of the (far) right. Great at mobilizing already politicized people against an amorphous overarching evil, but poor at coming up with a broadly supported positive agenda. Its mobilization is strongly facilitated by the infrastructure of previously existing social movements, which has provided a largely unstructured movement with a strong (inter)national media profile, but it is still a grassroots mobilization.

The 2014 GOP primaries will show whether the Tea Party was indeed just an AstroTurf invention, as many liberals have claimed, or whether it is, and always was, a true grassroots movement, as most conservatives proclaim. It will also show whether there still is a viable non-Tea Party GOP. Because even if big business *is* going to fund non- or even anti-Tea Party candidates, which isn't a foregone conclusion at all, there is no guarantee that these candidates will be able to win either the primaries or the actual election. After all, the problem is not necessarily mobilizing non-Tea Party GOP candidates, it is mobilizing non-Tea Party GOP activists and voters. Simply running as an anti-Tea Party Republican won't do the trick; it will probably get you money, it will definitely get you grassroots opposition, but it will probably not get you much grassroots support.

The real challenge for "moderate" Republicans, then, is to find an issue that will mobilize both "moderate" and "Tea Party" Republicans. More importantly, it should be an issue on which "moderate" Republicans can come across as more competent than "Tea Party" Republicans. This by and large excludes all negative issues, i.e. all issues based on opposition to something – be it Obamacare, raising the debt ceiling (again), immigration reform, or whatever – as the Tea Party will always be more consistent and extreme in their opposition. Traditionally, national security issues have been great for mainstream Republicans, but the GOP base has turned increasingly isolationist, and there is no credible threat to the homeland. Fiscal responsibility sounds great, but has so far not led to convincing policies, let alone a budget that could pass in Congress.

In short, the "moderate" GOP is increasingly a party with money but without (active) supporters. This might be enough to influence the public debate through expensive political campaigns, parroted by pundits on Fox News and other national media outlets, but is not enough to set the political agenda and dominate national policies. In contrast, the Tea Party might become a movement without (much) money but with an active mass base. Left to its own devices, i.e. deprived of (most) AstroTurf support, the Tea Party grassroots might lose its national agenda-setting powers, but can still be a major player at the local and regional levels – North Carolina provides a chilling example of what that looks like.

Notes

1 This chapter was first published in *Open Democracy* (28 October 2013).
2 See, among others, Lawrence Rosenthal and Christine Trost (eds), *Steep: The Precipitous Rise of the Tea Party* (Berkeley, CA: The University of California Press, 2012).

8 The Green Scare
Why Islamophobia is the new Red Scare

Since the terrorist attacks of 9/11 Islam has become the new enemy of the US right, which has led to a growing paranoia that increasingly resembles the infamous anti-communist "Red Scare" of the Cold War era.

While Islamophobia is nothing new to the West, clearly it has reached unprecedented heights in the post-9/11 era. Many Western European countries have radical right parties that promote strong Islamophobic policies, from banning the building of mosques (like the Swiss People's Party) to banning the Quran (like Dutch politician Geert Wilders). No strict Islamophobic parties exist in the United States, but a majority of the candidates in the 2012 Republican presidential primaries made anti-Islamic statements and hardly a week goes by without an Islamophobic event – from anti-Sharia law in North Carolina to no-Muslim parking in Houston.

It has been common to see Islamophobia as just the latest incarnation of racism or xenophobia, an irrational fear and prejudice towards a certain "ethnic" (or "racial" in the Anglo-Saxon world) group. Many commentators have named it the new anti-Semitism, arguing that the Muslims are the Jews of the 21st century. While there are certainly classic xenophobic aspects involved, the "racist" perspective is too limited to be able to explain the broad popularity of Islamophobia. If it were "just" a new racism or anti-Semitism, it would have remained mainly confined to the political extremes, whereas Islamophobia is expressed – in more or less extreme terms – by a broad variety of mainstream actors, from three-time Italian Prime Minister Silvio Berlusconi through German social democratic banker Thilo Sarazin to British tabloid columnist Melanie Phillips.

Prejudices like racism and xenophobia are about inherent features of "others," those who are and never were like us. They are mostly feared because they are intrinsically different. They are not expected to change, as they are not considered to be able to shed their inherently different feature. A Jew is a Jew is a Jew, irrespective how assimilated he or she is, as Nazi Germany made painfully clear. This ethnic or racial "Other" is feared because he (less she) is threatening the cultural or racial purity of society. While xenophobia light is shared by large sections of Western societies, ethnic nationalist ideologies tend to attract only minor support.

Islamophobia is so effective because it combines ethnic prejudice with a perceived threat of "our way of life." Muslims are not so much feared because of their threat to the ethnic purity of Western nations, but because they are alleged to threaten the "Western" way of life. Consequently, Islamophobes can present themselves as good democrats and patriots, defending "Western democracy" and "the USA" rather than a more contentious ethnic nationalist vision of society.

It is in this essential threat that Islamophobia resembles anti-communism, the prime fear of the Cold War period. Despite the continuous threat of mutual annihilation and the various proxy wars, the Cold War was a good period for the West, defined by progress and stability. The enemy was clear, even though the "fifth column" caused some paranoia, and helped strengthen the sense of superiority of the West. When the Cold War ended, the short period of jubilance, with American (neo)conservative Francis Fukuyama proclaiming "the end of history," was soon followed by a void.[1] Without an external enemy, the West was forced into introspection, while its military alliance was without a purpose. It wouldn't take the North Atlantic Treaty Organization (NATO) long to find a new one. In the early 1990s, the first Iraq War, NATO rose from the ashes and found a new purpose in its struggle against "Global Islam." A decade later, 9/11 did the rest, providing the perfect excuse to neoconservatives and others to start a diffuse "war on terror" against a vague enemy, "Islamists" or "Jihadists."

Although Orientalist essentialisms were never far away, the main argument for the "war on terror," and the underlying Islamophobia, was the threat of Islam and Muslims to "our way of life." Just like the communists in the 20th century, the Islamists were out to destroy our way of life, because they "hate our freedom." They are aided by "the axis of evil," Bush's equivalent of Reagan's "evil empire," notably Afghanistan and Iran. But there were domestic enemies too, ranging from "sleeper cells" (not unlike the Russians in *The Americans*) to communist/Islamist groups to the inevitable "useful idiots," i.e. any native Westerners who do not accept the communist/Islamist danger. A perfect example of the Islamophobia as the new Red Scare argument is made in conservative columnist Mona Charen's book, *Useful Idiots: How Liberals Got it Wrong in the Cold War and Still Blame America First* (2003).

Just as with anti-communism, the political mainstream is united in its fear of "radical Islam," but divided over who to fear, i.e. where the boundaries between moderate and radical fall. On the center and left "moderate Islam" is accepted, and sometimes even supported, just as social democracy was in the 20th century. Politicians like George W. Bush and Tony Blair always made clear distinctions between "good" and "bad" Muslims. On the far right, all Muslims are suspect. Just as Joseph McCarthy attacked liberals as closet communists in the 1950s, Islamophobes like Frank Gaffney and Pamela Geller attack moderate Muslims as closet Jihadists. According to them, a Muslim is by definition anti-democratic and anti-Western.

While anti-Semitism is based on the idea of a small cabal of powerful Jews who rule the world (think *The Protocols of the Elderly of Zion*), Islamophobia shares the anti-communist conspiracy theory of a powerful global force, including some identifiable state sponsors, who work through a "fifth column" in the West – operating through sleeper cells and front-organizations – and the naïve or opportunistic help of "useful idiots." In the US, the John Birch Society is using its extensive experience during the Red Scare to fuel the current "Green Scare." Together with professional Islamophobes like Daniel Pipes and Robert Spencer, they espouse conspiracy theories of Islamist (more concretely, Muslim Brotherhood) infiltration of the Obama administration. Key targets include all prominent Arabs, whether Muslim or not – such as Huma Abedin, close advisor of Hillary Clinton and wife of disgraced politician Anthony Weiner – to those married to Muslims (like Grover Norquist) to people like CIA Director John Brennan, who is alleged to have secretly converted to Islam in Saudi Arabia years ago. Just as the JBS accused various American presidents of being either secret communists or "communist sympathizers" (from Eisenhower to Kennedy), contemporary Islamophobes present President Obama as the "Muslim-in-Chief," who is secretly destroying "our way of life" from within the White House.

Just like in the 1950s and 1960s, when anti-communist conspiracies were accepted by many within the political mainstream, with Republican Senator Joseph McCarthy as the prime example, Islamophobic conspiracy theories have gained a far greater level of acceptance than ethnic or racial prejudices have in the postwar period. In addition to the well-funded and well-read books and websites of professional Islamophobes like Pamela Geller and Daniel Pipes, Islamophobic conspiracies are regularly aired by hosts and guests on Fox News, and even inform Congressional hearings – such as the ones by Peter King, Republican Representative for Long Island. During the 2012 GOP primaries

Michelle Bachmann, Herman Cain, Newt Gingrich, Rick Perry and Rick Sanctorum made Islamophobic statements in one form or another; while Ron Paul and Mitt Romney did not make anti-Islam statements, they did not put too much effort into denouncing the Islamophobic statements of their fellow Republicans.

But just like anti-communist paranoia wasn't limited to conservatives, Islamophobia is not the exclusive property of the (far and mainstream) right side of the political spectrum. Within Europe former liberal heroes like Dutch politician Ayaan Hirshi Ali and the late Italian author Oriana Fallaci are among the most radical Islamophobes. Just in the past months American feminist author Joyce Carol Oates and British atheist historian Richard Dawkins were called out for Islamophobic tweets. And Islamophobic books like Bruce Bawer's *When Europe Slept: How Radical Islam is Destroying the West from Within* and Christopher Caldwell's *Reflections on the Revolution in Europe: Immigration, Islam and the West* received positive or uncritical reviews in prominent liberal outlets, including the *New York Review of Books* and *The Colbert Report*. Not to speak of "liberal" icon Bill Maher, who, under the guise of the New Atheism, has been a major voice of Islamophobia for years.

More than fifteen years after the terrorist attacks of 9/11 Islamophobia is stronger than ever. Islamophobic "think tanks" like the former US Ambassador to the UN John Bolton's Gatestone Institute and Gaffney's Center for Security Policy are closely connected to conservative media and politicians, pushing conspiracy theories like the alleged Muslim Brotherhood "fifth column" infiltration of the highest positions of US government. But while the Green Scare has led to a similar paranoia as the Red Scare in the last century, it has so far failed to mobilize large crowds. Islamophobic demonstrations, like the Global Rally for Humanity in 2016, have failed to attract more than a few dozen people at a few dozen locations around the country. Then again, perhaps Islamophobic Americans feel that they have enough voice in the state and federal legislatures to rely on parliamentary, rather than extra-parliamentary, politics.

Note

1 Francis Fukuyama first made his argument in the article "The End of History?," published in *The National Interest* in Summer 1989. He later developed it into a book, entitled *The End of History and The Last Man* (New York: The Free Press, 1992).

9 The Trump phenomenon and the European populist radical right

Much of the US media tries to understand Donald Trump through the prism of the European populist radical right. This chapter does so by focusing on Trump, Trumpism, and the Trumpista, but emphasizes the typical American characteristics of all three.[1]

As everyone will have noticed, the media cannot get enough of Donald Trump. Although we know on the basis of virtually every previous (GOP) primary that the front-runner a year before the election is nowhere to be seen around election time, media from the left to the right are arguing that Trump, or at least the newly invented "Trumpism," is here to stay.

At the same time, journalists and pundits are having a hard time getting a grip on the slippery billionaire. They have even looked across the US borders to understand Trump. The more ideological have claimed that Trump is a fascist, the more sensationalist have merely stated the same as a rhetorical question: "Is Donald Trump a fascist?" This claim is so preposterous that it doesn't deserve a serious response.

Of more interest is the comparison with Europe's contemporary far right parties, which has been made in various pieces, but was developed in most detail in a piece with the telling title "If You Want To Understand Donald Trump, Look To the Success of the European Far-Right" by Matthew Yglesias (*Vox*, 25 August 2016). In fact, around the world, the media are asking the question: Is Donald Trump America's Le Pen? While the question is in itself not uninteresting, the answers often obscure the complexity of the Trump phenomenon and the typical American characteristics of Trump, Trumpism, and the Trumpista.

Not surprisingly, Trump the persona has received much attention. From the *New York Times* to the *Washington Post*, Trump is likened to another billionaire who went from entrepreneur to politician: Silvio Berlusconi, one of the richest men in Italy who dominated Italian politics for more than two decades. However, Berlusconi is an exception among European populists. As money doesn't play a similarly important role in European politics, most politicians, populist or not, are not particularly rich. Contrary to Europe, the US doesn't lack for examples of very rich people who use their business acumen and wealth to launch a political career – think of Mitt Romney, Steve Forbes, or Carly Fiorina. Several commentators have linked Trump to Ross Perot, another goofy-looking billionaire with an anti-establishment appeal. This discussion is particularly focused on Trump's chances as a third-party candidate, a possibility that he has not explicitly ruled out. Perot won almost 19 percent of the vote in the 1992 presidential election, making him the most successful third-party candidate since Theodore Roosevelt in 1912. Although some disagree with the received wisdom that Perot cost the GOP the presidency in 1992, there is growing fear of Trump doing the same in 2016. However, while Trump has some similarity to Perot as a person, mostly being a fellow-billionaire, Trumpism is more like the "paleo-conservativism" of Pat Buchanan than the right-wing populism of Perot.

"Trumpism" is far too big a term for the incoherent and ever-shifting views of Trump. It is impossible to discern an ideology that Trump adheres to. He never developed a real ideological platform and has been inconsistent on core issues – from pro-choice to anti-abortion, from pro-universal healthcare to anti-Obamacare, etc. However, his current popularity does seem to be based on a combination of features that defines Europe's contemporary populist radical right: nativism, authoritarianism, and populism. Just like politicians such as Geert Wilders in the Netherlands – whose main campaign poster reads: "More Security. Less Immigration" – Trump links immigration and crime in his speeches. He thereby plays on widespread beliefs that illegal immigration is causing an increase in serious crime.

However, his general views on immigration and integration are much more in line with US conservatives than with the European far right. For instance, Trump singles out illegal immigration and does not attack the status of the US as a multicultural immigration country. And while he has been speaking about "the Muslim problem" at least since 2011, he is much more nuanced in his views of Islam and Muslims than people like Marine Le Pen and, certainly, Geert Wilders. In fact, his views on Muslims really don't stand out much from many other prominent Republicans – a majority of the main candidates in the 2012 GOP primary made Islamophobic statements.

Paradoxically, the term most often used to describe Trump, both in the US and abroad, is possibly the most problematic: populism. There is no doubt that Trump is an anti-establishment candidate. He has called all (other) politicians incompetent and corrupt, including virtually all of his competitors in the GOP primary. But populism entails not just an anti-elite position, which is common to most political challengers, but also a pro-people position and a call for "common-sense" politics. A real populist is the *vox populi* (voice of the people) because he or she is one of the people. Think of Sarah Palin, who referred to herself as an "average hockey mom."

There is nothing average about Donald Trump, according to Donald Trump. His speeches are replete with self-complimentary anecdotes and references to himself in the third person. The message is not a humble "I am like you," but rather a grandiose "become another Trump." He doesn't even really need "the people" to "Make America Great Again" (his campaign slogan). The Donald will make America great again, because, as his campaign website says, "Donald J. Trump is the very definition of the American success story, continually setting the standards of excellence."

Contrary to the man (Trump) and the ideology (Trumpism), the supporter of Trump (the Trumpista) is almost identical to the populist radical right voter in (Western) Europe. First studies show that Trump is particularly popular among young, lower-educated, white males.[2] This is exactly the same group that constitutes the core of the electorate of populist radical right parties in Western Europe. The gender gap is particularly striking. Just as European populist radical right parties have a much larger gender gap than mainstream right-wing parties, attracting roughly two men for every one woman, Trump has the largest gender gap among the GOP candidates, particularly among likely Republican primary voters. And while Trump has claimed that he is the only Republican who can win the Hispanic vote, surveys show that he is by far the least-liked GOP candidate among Hispanics.

In conclusion, to understand the Trump phenomenon in all its complexity we need to look at both US history and contemporary Europe. *Trumpismo* can be seen as a functional equivalent of the European populist radical right, but it is a very American equivalent. Trump himself doesn't hold a populist radical right ideology, but his political campaign clearly caters to populist radical right attitudes, and his supporter base is almost identical to the core electorate of populist radical right parties in (Western) Europe. However, Trump also stands in a long tradition of American nativism (see Chapter 2), going back to the Know Nothings of the mid 19th century, of American anti-establishment politicians, and of conservatives who claim to be the right "CEO" to make America great again. But, in contrast to the rich history of US populism, Trump is an anti-establishment elitist. *He* is better than everyone, i.e. both the elite and the people!

Notes

1 This chapter was first published in the *Washington Post* (26 August 2015).
2 See Emily Ekins, "Here's the Lowdown on Who Supports Donald Trump," *The Federalist*, 5 August 2016, available at: http://thefederalist.com/2015/08/05/heres-the-lowdown-on-who-supports-donald-trump/ (last visited on 1 May 2017).

10 The power of populism?
Not really!

According to the media, populist candidates are challenging the establishments of both the Democratic Party and the Republican Party. But are Bernie Sanders and Donald Trump really populists?[1]

Journalists and pundits had been waiting for it for months: a win for Sanders and Trump in the same primary. Then they could finally rehash their "rise of populism" articles, which they had already published a few months earlier when Sanders and Trump first emerged as possibly relevant candidates. And we were not disappointed after the New Hampshire primaries: from "How Rising Trump and Sanders Parallel Rising Populism in Europe" (*Huffington Post*) to "New Hampshire Primary Results Underscore the Power of Populism" (*The Star*) and "The Populists Are On Top" (*The Economist*), the message was loud and clear: there is a new sheriff in town, populism, and it is ruling supreme in US politics. But is it? And, if so, is that new(s)?

10.1 What is populism?

The answer depends partly, as so often, on definitions. Most commentators don't define populism and mainly refer to "anti-establishment positions" and "simplistic solutions" – in other words, to political campaigning. There is nothing new about this, of course, particularly not in the US. So let's use a definition that actually distinguishes populism from broader phenomena like demagogy and political campaigning. Populism is *an ideology that considers society to be ultimately separated into two homogeneous and antagonistic groups, "the pure people" and "the corrupt elite," and which argues that politics should be an expression of the* volonté générale *(general will) of the people.*[2]

This definition is quite similar to the one US historian Michael Kazin uses in his seminal book *The Populist Persuasion: An American*

History (1998). Like most scholars of populism, Kazin considers the People's Party of the late 19th century as the original populist movement. He shows how populist sentiments have always been deeply rooted in US society, being exploited in time by both mainstream politicians – think about Richard Nixon's "silent majority" – and populist upstarts – none more popular than Texas billionaire Ross Perot.

10.2 Populism in the early 21st century

The 21st century has seen an explosion of populism across the globe, from left populist presidents like Rafael Correa and Hugo Chávez in Latin America to right populist parties like Forza Italia (FI) and the National Front (FN) in Europe. The US has not been immune to populism either this century. After all, it was just a few years ago that (in part the same) pundits announced the "rise of populism" with regard to Occupy Wall Street and the Tea Party!

In many ways Sanders and Trump are the party political voices of these two movements. Not that either was a part of either movement, but they express very similar sentiments and find support among people who were part of, or at least supportive of, them. Many of Sanders's critiques of the role of banks in the Great Recession and of the influence of money in politics are similar to those voiced at Zuccotti Park. And many of Trump's critiques of the GOP establishment and the Obama administration were part and parcel of the Tea Party in its many permutations. However, Trump is more the voice of the Tea Party grassroots, which was always more authoritarian and nativist than the business-dominated AstroTurf.

But despite all the similarities there are important differences between Sanders and Occupy Wall Street, and Trump and the (grassroots) Tea Party. One of the most important is related to populism. While Occupy and the Tea Party were essentially populist movements, neither Sanders nor Trump is a populist. Yes, you read that right: neither Sanders nor Trump is a populist!

10.3 Sanders, the confused social democrat

The core of Occupy Wall Street's populist message was not just the division of society between "the 99 percent" and "the 1 percent," but the morality of that division. *The* 99 percent was good, pure, and *the* 1 percent was bad, corrupt. Occupy did acknowledge distinctions within the 99 percent, accommodating most notably gender and race, but these divisions were in the end secondary to the overarching *moral* struggle against the homogeneous 1 percent. It was a ultimately a struggle of values, not interests.

While Sanders regularly rails against "the 1 percent," he seldom identifies himself with "the 99 percent." More importantly, the main division in Sanders's discourse is one of *interest*, i.e. of class struggle, not morality. When he criticizes that the top 0.1 percent of US society have almost as much wealth as the bottom 90 percent, he deplores the morality of that *situation* rather than of the 0.1 percent. Incidentally, he does so based on solid studies. His critique is mostly institutional rather than individual. For example, he vows to take on "the greed" of "corporate America" and of "Wall Street." This perfectly fits with his overarching ideological narrative – which he misguidedly calls "democratic socialism," but is actually pretty classic social democracy – which is built around class interests.

10.4 Trump: the elitist anti-establishment candidate of the people

Similarly, Trump has adopted part of the populist message of the Tea Party, criticizing both the Democratic and Republican establishments for incompetence and for being in the pockets of big donors. He also rails against an alleged liberal "political correctness" and claims to break "political taboos" like illegal immigration – as if we haven't just had years of nativist discourse surrounding the various anti-immigration legislation starting with SB1070 in Arizona in 2010. Like many Republicans before him, including presidents Nixon and Reagan, Trump claims to speak for "the silent majority" that wants to "take our country back" (from whom remains a bit unclear).

However, whereas Trump is clear on the corruption, although even more incompetence, of the homogeneous elite, making little distinction between Democrats and Republicans, he only heralds "the people" when he thinks they support him. Overall, he speaks little about the virtues of "the people." What Trump speaks about, over and over again, is Trump. Where populist leaders claim to be the *vox populi*, the voice of the people, Trump is the voice of Trump. He does not claim to follow the wisdom of the people, as an integral part of that homogeneous people. He argues that *he* is the best CEO for "America" because *he* has unique skills and experiences.

In typical elitist fashion The Donald claims to be different, and yes better, than the (common) people. Note this recent statement on *Meet the Press* on January 24, 2016: "I am a conservative, but I get along with people." Leaving aside his (unconvincing) claim to conservatism, he implicitly separates himself, and conservatives more generally, from (the) people. Trump doesn't claim to be "one of the people," as (real) populists do, but that, *despite the fact that he is different*, people love him. And while he here implicitly refers to white people, the bulk of his base, he uses similar language with regard to ethnic minorities, from Hispanics to African Americans, who all "love" him (despite that he is different from them).

This is all not to say that populism is not underlying some of the support for both Sanders and Trump – it is. But there is nothing new to that. In fact, one could argue that it simply reflects the broader movement that Occupy Wall Street and the Tea Party started a few years ago. More important, however, is that neither Sanders nor Trump is a populist politician. Sanders is an American social democrat, mixing American and European traditions of progressive politics, while Trump is the latest of that all-American brand of businessman savior – well, at least until Michael Bloomberg jumps into the race. Hence, while using the term populism might help taint their campaigns, and sell newspapers, it does not help us that much in understanding the true political programs of these two politicians.

Notes

1 This chapter was first published in the *Huffington Post* (13 February 2016).
2 I have developed this understanding of populism together with Cristóbal Rovira Kaltwasser in our book *Populism: A Very Short Introduction* (New York: Oxford University Press, 2017).

11 Is the GOP a far right party?

The Republican Party has been categorized as a mainstream, conservative political party for decades. But many of the frontrunners in its 2016 primaries are pushing conservatism to its extremes, making the question of whether the party itself might be(come) far right increasingly relevant.[1]

I know what you are thinking ... no, of course not. After all, the Republican Party, or Grand Old Party (GOP), is a party of the right, conservative, but square within the political mainstream. Just because Donald Trump is leading the primaries, and the GOP seems unable and unwilling to stop him, does not make the whole party far right. The official Republican Platform of 2016 is more or less mainstream conservative, as is the (toothless) party leader Reince Priebus. And only a minority of the party's members of Congress, most notably in the House of Representatives, is ideologically far right – such as Michelle Bachmann (Minnesota), Louie Gohmert (Texas), Steve King (Iowa), and Jeff Sessions (Alabama).

The situation is much less clear at the state level, however. Here authoritarianism and nativism run rampant among governors and legislators alike. It is almost exclusively among GOP-controlled states that strict anti-immigration and "anti-Sharia" legislation was introduced. And the vast majority of Republican governors refused to accept Syrian refugees to their state, on the unfounded allegation that they would include terrorists.

American parties are not the centralized, homogenous political organizations that European parties are. The particular combination of a first-past-the-post electoral system and extremely expensive campaigns means that individuals can create some independence vis-à-vis national party leaders, particularly if they have their own financial backers or sources. Consequently, the parties are strongly influenced by some individual members, particularly if one of those individuals wins the presidency. In other words, the major presidential candidates play a major role in the (self-)characterization of the party.

The real problem of the GOP today is that Donald Trump is not just a far right outsider, who has infiltrated a mainstream right-wing party, as the establishment is desperately trying to tell you and most mainstream media continue to confirm. The success of Trump is in many ways *the product* of a decade-long radicalization of the grassroots and cadres of the party and, consequently, Trump represents the party at least as much as Senate majority leader Mitch McConnell or failed establishment candidate Jeb Bush.

The case for labeling Trump "far right" is pretty straightforward. The core of his campaign is authoritarianism and nativism fueled with fierce and vulgar anti-establishment rhetoric. No minority is safe from him: Mexicans, Muslims, African Americans, and even Jews – who were treated to beautiful examples of anti-Semitic philosemitism, including the already legendary "I'm a negotiator, like you folks," at a speech to the Republican Jewish Coalition last year. For Trump every issue is, in essence, a security issue that has to be dealt with in an authoritarian manner – from the wall with Mexico to terrorism – in which he does not shy away from using violence (including torture). Not surprising then that authoritarianism is a key factor explaining support for Trump among voters. While he is not a true populist (see Chapter 10), as he believes in his own unique virtues and not those of the (common) people, his anti-establishment discourse is very similar to that of far right populists in Europe, i.e. claiming all elites are essentially corrupt and on the same side.

The problem for the GOP is that Trump is not the only major candidate whose core beliefs are at odds with liberal democracy, in particularly minority rights. Each of the remaining five presidential candidates has proposed to limit the rights of minorities such as gays and Muslims. In fact, the top three candidates have all called for increased monitoring of "Muslim communities" in sharp opposition to religious freedom and, obviously, the First Amendment.

In fact, if the 2016 primaries had been normal by any conventional standard, even the standards of the 2012 GOP primaries (which were also littered with religious extremism and Islamophobia), all the attention and outrage would have been focused on the behavior and ideas of Ted Cruz. And I am not talking about him cooking bacon with a machine gun. Cruz has a long and well-established track record of supporting far right causes and conspiracies. In a recent article in the SPLC's *Intelligence Report* (Winter 2015) on the ten most popular far right conspiracy theories in the United States, Cruz featured regularly as one of the most prominent supporters of those theories – including the insane conspiracies around Agenda 21, an alleged attempt to put "the tentacles of the UN into US institutions" (one of the key conspiracy theories of the far right John Birch Society), and Jade Helm, the 2015 US military training exercise in several Southern states that many far right activists in Texas thought was a secret Pentagon plan to invade their state.

And, despite Trump's recent re-invention as a devout Christian, uncritically accepted by a large portion of the Religious Right, the real religious extremism comes from other candidates within the party, most notably Ben Carson and Ted Cruz. Asked "a simple question" on MSNBC (1 May 2016), namely, "Does the Bible have authority over the Constitution?," Carson answered "That is not a simple question," arguing that it depended on the "specific context." Cruz has said, on multiple occasions, "[t]hat our rights do not come from the Democratic Party or the Republican Party or even from the Tea Party. Our rights come from our creator."[2] In other words, two of the five remaining GOP presidential candidates believe that the Bible is more important than the Constitution, which suggests a theocratic understanding of politics that is directly at odds with democracy, not just liberal democracy.

Even the last hope of the GOP establishment, Marco Rubio, is not a traditional mainstream conservative. First, he was catapulted into national politics by the Tea Party movement, even though he quickly abandoned them when he found other, richer backers. Second, he has supported classic far right tropes, such as the denial of man-made climate change or the obviously wrong assertion that Christianity is being treated as "hate speech" under President Obama. In one of the most bizarre moments in the campaign so far, a very high bar, Rubio and Cruz, both Cuban Americans, were trying to out-Trump each other on immigration, with Rubio outright denying his previous support for immigration reform and blurring lines between immigrants and terrorists. Similarly, there is little light between Rubio's anti-Muslim comments and those of Trump (or Cruz). In fact, after Trump had stated that mosques should be under surveillance because of the risk of "radical Islam," Rubio extended that to "any place – whether it's a cafe, a diner, an internet site – any place where radicals are being inspired."[3]

So, what does this say about the GOP today? Is *the* GOP a far right party? Clearly not if one only looks at the official front of the party, i.e. the fairly irrelevant party leader and platform. And only at the margins if one looks at the main (national) representatives in US Congress. But increasingly, if one focuses on the most popular candidates for presidency, who, if successful, will be the most powerful person within the party. Consequently, it is high time that the GOP leadership and supporters who do still support liberal democracy take responsibility and see their party for what it is. Not a party that was hijacked by Trump (and Cruz), but a party that created him, and which is now increasingly shaped in his image.

Notes

1 This chapter was first published in the *Huffington Post* (28 February 2016).
2 See, for instance, Dana Lind, "Iowa Caucus: Ted Cruz Echoes Ronald Reagan in Victory Speech," *Vox*, 2 February 2016, available at: www.vox.com/2016/2/2/10892740/ted-cruz-iowa-caucus-speech (last visited on 1 May 2017).
3 Kay Steiger, "Rubio Trumps Trump: Shut Down Any Place Muslims Gather To Be 'Inspired' – Not Just Mosques," *ThinkProgress*, 20 November 2015, available at: https://thinkprogress.org/rubio-trumps-trump-shut-down-any-place-muslims-gather-to-be-inspired-not-just-mosques-a83a986f86a4 (last visited on 1 May 2017).

12 Will Donald Trump transform the (far) right in the US?

This (Super) Tuesday Donald Trump took another big step closer to the Republican nomination for the 2016 presidential election. But what will his nomination do to and for the (far) right in the US? Will Trump leave a far right legacy?[1]

This week was another Super Tuesday and, just like the previous one, two weeks earlier, all the attention went to Donald Trump, the big winner in the camp of the Republican Party – also known as the Grand Old Party (GOP). By now, there is no longer any doubt that Trump is serious about his presidential run and that he will win the most votes in the GOP primaries. Even more importantly, he will win the most delegates for the GOP convention, which will make the final decision on who the official party candidate for the 2016 presidential election will be.

While it is almost certain that Trump will win a majority of primaries and caucuses and a plurality of delegates, Texas Senator Ted Cruz will secure enough delegates to keep Trump from a majority. This will mean that no candidate will get the nomination in the first vote, after which the delegates are no longer bound to "their" candidate. And here the so-called "brokered convention," which the GOP desperately tries to rebrand as "open convention" to make it sound less elitist and more democratic, comes into play. It is no secret that the vast majority of the GOP establishment despises Trump and believes that he would ruin the party. However, no one likes Cruz either, who is held responsible for the unpopular government shutdown of 2013. Given that the eventual nominee does not have to be one of the 17 candidates who started the primaries, the names of other GOP heavyweights, including House Speaker Paul Ryan and failed 2012 presidential candidate Mitt Romney, have been rumored as possible options.

It is clear that Trump holds the GOP elite in a chokehold and its masses in a spell. Whether he gets the nomination or not, Trump has defined the 2016 presidential race in more ways than one. First of all, he has set the tone and the issues of the campaign. Trump mainly talks about three things: himself (good), all other politicians (bad), and all "outsiders" (very bad). He has called Mexican immigrants "rapists" and referred to Syrian refugees as "snakes." He sends thousands of people into a frenzy at his sold-out rallies, which are increasingly meetings of intimidation and (verbal) violence. Trump has openly encouraged this, for example when he said about an African American Black Lives Matter activist, who had disrupted one of his rallies: "maybe he should have been roughed up." He even asked his supporters to raise their hand and pledge allegiance to him, providing even more fuel to the accusations that he is a fascist.

While Trump lacks the ideological coherence and organizational structure of fascism, his unabashed nativism and explicit intimidation of critics and support for violence are unprecedented in recent US history. In fact, they even set him apart from most serious populist radical right politicians in Europe, such as Marine Le Pen or Geert Wilders, despite the fact that they have expressed support for Trump and rightly see him as a kindred spirit. Trump has also revived the US white nationalist subculture from the dead. Most American racists have embraced the billionaire real estate mogul on social media and several have attended his rallies or are actively campaigning on his behalf (though without his explicit approval).

Whether Trump gets the nomination or not, he is destined to fail in the presidential election. While he is by far the most-liked candidate within the Republican field, he is also the most disliked, both within the Republican field and among all voters. No presidential candidate has such high unfavorability ratings, not even Hillary Clinton, who for many Republicans is the anti-Christ. So, if Trump is nominated, many moderate Republicans will either not vote, or vote for the Democratic candidate. Alternatively, when he is kept from the nomination by a brokered convention, Trump will either run as a third candidate or will tell his supporters not to vote at all. Either way, the GOP will lose the 2016 presidential election and will blame Trump.

But Trump is a symptom of broader GOP problems rather than the cause of them. The primaries have exposed a huge gap between the party establishment and the party supporters, who have shown no interest in establishment candidates like Jeb Bush and Marco Rubio. In fact, almost two-thirds of Republicans support either Trump or Cruz, both far right candidates. While Trump is more similar to the populist radical right in Europe, although more elitist than populist – virtue resides in The Donald, not the people (see Chapter 10) – Cruz is a more typical American phenomenon, combining small government and Constitutional extremism with theocratic sentiments – for example, he holds the Bible above the Constitution. His views are more similar to some small fundamentalist Protestant groups in Europe, like the Politically Reformed Party (SGP) in the Netherlands or factions of the Democratic Unionist Party (DUP) in Northern Ireland.

So, what will Trump's political legacy be? Given that he is a one-man show, who has not shown any interest in building a more permanent organization, he will probably leave little institutional legacy within the GOP or outside it. Once he loses the nomination or the presidential election, he will disappear from politics, and so will the "Trump Movement." But other GOP politicians will be inspired by his success, particularly in the (Deep) South, where Trump has destroyed his competitors. They will continue the nativist "Southern Strategy" at the state and local levels, even if the national GOP will probably try to move away from it and adopt a more inclusive strategy that targets, in particular, religious Hispanic voters.

His main legacy will be outside the GOP, however. As said, the marginal and splintered white nationalist subculture has been rejuvenated by the Trump phenomenon, experiencing a growth in interest and membership. While this will not lead to the formation of a serious political movement, let alone a party, it could further boost the radicalization of far right groups, from white nationalists to anti-government "sovereign citizens" (such as the ones involved in the Oregon stand-off), and with it the danger of more violence. This is even more so if Trump is stopped by the GOP elite (brokered convention), instead of the American people (presidential election), as this could provide the (violent) US far right with its own *Dolchstoss Legende* (Stab in the Back Myth).

Note

[1] This chapter was first published in *HOPE not hate Magazine* (March–April 2016).

13 Donald Trump
The Great White Hope

While Donald Trump presents himself as a typical American phenomenon, rallying behind the slogan "America First," most American accounts see him primarily as a foreign or un-American phenomenon. However, Trump is in many ways as American as apple pie, standing in a long tradition of authoritarian, nativist and populist politics in the United States.[1]

It is intriguing that the rise of Donald Trump is mostly analyzed with a comparative European framework, given the usually parochial nature of US public debate. Whereas global values like democracy and freedom are usually described as "American values," Donald Trump is, implicitly or explicitly, portrayed as "un-American" – a European *Fremdkörper* (foreign body) in the pure American democratic polity. Hence, in the thousands of stories about "the Trump phenomenon" confused US readers hear more about Adolf Hitler, Silvio Berlusconi and Marine Le Pen than about Huey Long, George Wallace, and Pat Buchanan.

13.1 The radical right as a pathological normalcy

While there is much to be learned from contemporary European developments, rather than historical ones, this one-sided frame obscures at least as much as it highlights. It paints Trump as an aberration of American history and strengthens the misperception that Americans are (the only) true liberal democrats, who have built a multicultural democratic utopia, while Europeans continue to be at best problematic democrats, who can barely control their nationalist demons – a view held by many Americans, as I experience first-hand each time a fresh class of college students takes my courses on European politics or on far right politics in Western democracies.

The uncomfortable truth is that the radical right has a long history in both Europe and the US, and that radical right values are not a "normal pathology" of Western democratic values, as was argued most famously within the US by the great historian Richard Hofstadter, but a "pathological normalcy," a radicalization of mainstream values (see in more detail in Chapter 25).

13.2 The Trump phenomenon: moving target and blurred vision

The main problem with understanding the Trump phenomenon is that Trump is an ever-moving target that we are studying with blurred vision. Trump has held contrasting views on most key issues (e.g. abortion and guns) and people (e.g. Hillary Clinton) in US politics. On top of that, his rise is still quite recent and without a clear precedent, which makes it not just hard to predict where it will end, but also to study what it *is*.

To fully understand the Trump phenomenon we have to look at three related, but distinct, aspects: the actor, the ideology, and the supporters (see Chapter 10). If we put these in a broader comparative and historical perspective, we find that Trump is as much part of a specific US historical tradition as he is part of a broader contemporary "Western" trend. And while no specific aspect is truly new, the overall Trump phenomenon as such is unique and without a clear contemporary or historical equivalent. Something "The Donald" himself would surely agree with.

13.3 Trump the (political) actor

Not surprisingly, most attention in the "analyses" of the Trump phenomenon has focused on the person of Donald Trump. In particular, his personality and wealth, exaggerated or not, have inspired European comparisons. Probably the most popular is with former Italian Prime Minister Silvio Berlusconi, who also combines excessive riches with a strong media profile – although Berlusconi literally owns most Italian media rather than just figuratively like Trump – and a desire to be surrounded by beautiful young(er) women.

Obviously, Trump's personality and wealth are an important part of the Trump phenomenon, as they not only attract supporters but also journalists. The mainstream media would never have devoted such disproportionate attention to him without his high media profile *before* entering politics. But these features define Trump more as a media personality than as a political actor.

As a political actor Trump is actually a very uncommon case. Sure, we have seen more than enough old, rich, white men in politics, but most would either challenge the system from outside the mainstream parties, founding their own new party (e.g. Berlusconi, Pim Fortuyn, or Ross Perot), or run within the mainstream parties and not challenge the system (e.g. GOP predecessor Mitt Romney or Finnish PM Juha Sipila). What sets Trump apart from almost all other "anti-establishment" politicians, in Europe or Latin America, is that he has mounted his challenge from *within* the establishment parties.

But Trump is not only an anti-establishment candidate within an establishment party, he is technically also a leader without a party – just as the GOP is a party without a leader. While the GOP establishment is increasingly embracing the same man they have accused of "hijacking" and "destroying" their party for the last months, Trump is much less popular among the GOP establishment than among the GOP (primary) voters. And Trump has so far done little to strengthen his grip on the party organization, let alone build a political organization outside the GOP.

To a certain extent this odd situation is a consequence of the unique US party system, dominated by two stable, but weakly centralized and organized, political parties. But it also reflects the contemporary political context, in which traditional party structures have become much less important for mobilizing supporters; particularly if you have the (social and traditional) media visibility of Trump, who has a staggering 8.43 million followers on Twitter and has dominated the major networks since the start of the primaries.

13.4 Trumpism: a proto-ideology

Although "Trumpism" is not a particularly coherent or developed ideology, it has some consistent and dominant ideological features. Its core is a combination of nativism, authoritarianism, and anti-establishment sentiments, which is very similar, though not identical, to the core ideology of the European populist radical right.

Trump directs his nativist attacks primarily at immigrants and refugees, first Latinos and later also Muslims. He combines it with a slightly less overt racism, against African Americans and even native Americans – recount his "Pocahontas" comment to Senator Elizabeth Warren. In line with authoritarianism Trump defines most social problems in terms of authority and security, and proposes (only) strict law and order solutions – from needing "a little bit more" punching of (non-violent) demonstrations to torture to prevent (jihadi) terrorism. While he shares nativism and authoritarianism with the European radical right, this is not the case for populism (see also Chapter 9). Trump does argue that "the elite" are all corrupt and the same, but he does not exalt the virtues of "the (pure) people." In the end, Trump is not the *vox populi* (voice of the people) but the *vox Donaldus* (voice of The Donald).

It is important to stress that these are not just constructions of the Trump campaign, concocted by focus groups and sinister political advisors. All are clearly core features of Trump's worldview, as we know from many statements from before his presidential run. For example, in the aftermath of the brutal rape of a (white) jogger in Central Park in 1989, Trump took out a full-page ad in four local newspapers with the title "Bring Back the Death Penalty! Bring Back the Police!" When the so-called Central Park Five (all young, non-white males) were finally exonerated, Trump called the city settlement with them "a disgrace."

The features that constitute Trumpism have a long history in the United States. Well before fascism reared its ugly head in Europe, the Know Nothings had unleashed violent nativist campaigns in various cities across the country. And in the 20th century American proto-fascists like Father Coughlin and the America First Party – not accidentally Trump emphasized "America First" in his first big foreign policy speech – had broad support, as did third-party candidates like George Wallace and Ross Perot (see Chapter 2). While none was identical to Trump or Trumpism, they often shared as many features as the contemporary European radical right – let alone historical European fascism, which was a profoundly different phenomenon.

13.5 The Trump supporters: the angry white working class?

It is not so easy to speak of *the* Trump supporter, let alone compare *him* to *the* European radical right supporter. Different European parties have partly different electorates. At the same time, Trump's electoral base is not yet well-studied and still shifting. As Trump becomes more defined and redefined, his supporters group grows and changes. Moreover, as the presumptive Republican presidential candidate, the "Trump vote" is becoming more and more a loyal GOP vote. Consequently, the "Trump vote" is starting to divert even more from the typical "radical right vote" in parliamentary elections in Europe. In November it will probably be more similar to the "Hofer vote" in the second round of the Austrian presidential elections, combining a radical right with a broader right and protest vote.

The stereotypical view of the radical right electorate is that of the angry white working-class male. This stereotype has dominated media coverage at least since the 1980s and has been equally prominent with regard to Trump. While there is some empirical basis to this view, it is mostly a self-serving elitist interpretation of popular(ized) social science. In its most elitist interpretation, white working-class males are the "fearful and frustrated" who vote for the radical right because they cannot cope with the economic and social transformations that accompany "globalization." Intellectually limited and rigid, they deal with their loss of "privilege" by "clinging" to a comforting "imagined community" and "scapegoating" minorities. In a more sympathetic account, white working-class males have been the objective "losers of globalization," politically abandoned by social democratic parties, who support the one group of parties that still (claim to) defend their interests.

There is truth in both interpretations, but they address only part of the broader electoral support base of successful radical right actors, including Trump in the US. Any party or politician with an electorate of 20 percent or more of the population has inevitably a fairly diverse support base. While white working-class males constitute an important and disproportionate part, they comprise just a minority. Whether it is really true that Trump (and Tea Party) supporters are richer than the average American, the naked truth is that white working-class males are too small a part of the US electorate to bring any political candidate to prominence.

13.6 Donald Trump: an essentially American phenomenon

At a basic level, the Trump phenomenon is part of a broader nativist, authoritarian, anti-establishment movement that neoliberal globalization has unleashed around the world. But this broad and vague "backlash theory" explains only a small part of the rise of Marine Le Pen, ISIS, or Trump (see Chapter 16). To truly understand each of these phenomena, we should look at both general international and specific national factors and traditions. In its essence, the Trump phenomenon is at least as much American as it is European.

Trump stands in a long US tradition of right-wing businessmen who present themselves as saviors of "the American way" and who can attract cross-class coalitions of supporters – including, among others, Henry Ford, Robert W. Welch Jr, and Ross Perot. Trumpism also shares many features with distinctly American ideologies, expressed through organizations like the Know Nothings in the mid-19th century, George Wallace in the mid-20th century, and the Tea Party movement in the early 21st century (see Chapter 2).

At the same time, Trump is unique, in both a contemporary and historical American and European context, in that he is an anti-establishment "outsider" who mobilizes through an establishment party. This aspect is often underemphasized, particularly by the obsession with European comparisons. Berlusconi and Le Pen had to fight to get *into* the political mainstream, while Trump's fight was from the start *within* the political mainstream. It was largely *because* he was running within the GOP primary race that he received the generous media attention – it is doubtful he would have received anything near that attention had he entered the race as an independent third-party candidate.

Consequently, the rise of Trump is closely linked to recent developments within and around the Grand Old Party. While establishment Republicans accuse Trump of having hijacked "their" party, the truth is that the party had started its decisive shift to the far right well before he entered the 2016 primaries. In fact, this shift even predates the rise of the Tea Party movement, of which the Trump phenomenon is, to a certain extent, a powerful aftershock.

Although European comparisons are insightful, in part because the European radical right is much better studied than the US radical right, they have only limited value and can serve as a convenient way to white-wash US history. By taking the US history and traditions of radical right politics more seriously, we will not only learn more about the Trump phenomenon, but also about the strengths *and weaknesses* of liberal democracy in the United States.

Note

1 A shorter, and very different, version of this chapter was published as "As American as Trump" in *Boston Review* (13 June 2016).

14 A talk with Cas Mudde on American and European populism

The website Political Observer of Populism (POP) interviewed Prof. Cas Mudde about populism in the US and Europe, the presence (or rather absence) of populism in the current American presidential campaign, and the conditions triggering different types of populism in the Old continent. Are "the people" and "the elites" relevant categories in the discourses articulated by Trump and Sanders? The economic crisis, combined with terrorist threats and a constant flow of migrants, create a widespread fear among the European electorate: which political actors benefit from this situation? These and other issues in the interview with Prof. Mudde. Enjoy ...[1]

POP: 1 *The New Yorker* (10 February 2016) titles "Bernie Sanders and Donald Trump Ride the Populist Wave," and the US edition of the *Huffington Post* (2 October 2016) echoes "How Rising Trump and Sanders Parallel Rising Populism in Europe." I am absolutely, 100 percent sure that if I claim that Trump and Sanders are populist I will appear as a smart and well-informed commentator. Correct?

CM: Yes, you would give the journalists what they want, namely a simplistic interpretation of contemporary politics, in which all politics is reduced to mainstream versus populism. However, you would not be correct according to some definitions, including my own. I believe neither Trump nor Sanders is populist (see Chapter 10). Trump doesn't speak in the name of the people, but (only) in the name of The Donald, and Sanders has fundamentally an interest-based discourse, not a normative discourse.

POP: 2 What do Trump and Sanders consider being their "enemy," and what do they mean when they refer to "the people"?

CM: Neither politician speaks much about "the enemy," but they do distinguish an "elite." For Sanders this is "the 1 percent," echoing the Occupy Wall Street movement, which has integrated this terminology into political mainstream. It is mostly the super-rich, linked specifically to Wall Street, who control US politicians because of the role of "big money" in US politics. For Trump it is a combination of Wall Street and East Coast liberals, thereby following the longstanding interpretation of "the elite" of right-wing populism in the US, most recently expressed by the Tea Party movement. For Sanders the people are "the working people" or "the middle class" (which in the US normally means the working class). He describes them mainly in terms of interests and basic values (e.g. hard work), but his discourse is not ultimately normative. He also draws upon the abundance of academic research that proves that the richest 1 percent of Americans have profited from most of the economic recovery since 2008. Trump refers to an amorphous "the people," which are mostly the ones that are "screwed" by the elites. They are innocent and gullible rather than a moral compass.

POP: 3 Can we say that Trump took over part of the Tea Party message, while Sanders is continuing the discourse articulated by Occupy Wall Street?

CM: Yes, even though neither was really part of those movements. Trump taps into the anger of the Tea Party grassroots, which was always authoritarian and nativist, while openly attacking the Tea Party AstroTurf, which is closely allied to the Republican establishment. But his socio-economic agenda is somewhat different from the Tea Party, in most of its versions, as he stands for a stronger role of the government in certain aspects (e.g. health care and tariffs). Sanders has taken on many of the issues, and seemingly supporters, of the Occupy movement, without necessarily its leaders. His movement is quite white and middle class, but Sanders combines it with an old-school social democratic agenda, which reflects his own youth rather than that of its young supporters.

POP: 4 But then, does it still make sense to speak of populism when analyzing the US presidential campaign? In other words, if Trump and Sanders are not populist, is there anyone among the candidates who could be labeled as such?

CM: No.

POP: 5 One-million-dollar question: how could Clinton ever lose against Sanders first and Trump then? What could turn the campaign in another direction?

CM: She can't, really. Because of the undemocratic internal system of the Democratic primaries, Sanders is doomed. In fact, he would probably have even lost, although slightly, in a more democratically (proportional) organized primary. She could lose against Trump, however unlikely this is. I see two vulnerabilities: 1 a major new scandal involving the Clintons (always possible given the past and present of them and the Clinton Foundation); and 2 a major terrorist attack on the US close to the election.

POP: 6 In a famous (more quoted than read) article published in 2004, you described the success of populist parties referring to a populist Zeitgeist.[2] Is the Zeitgeist still alive and kicking in 2016?

CM: Hmmm, I don't know how I feel about it being more quoted than read ... both have advantages, I guess. Anyway, yes, the populist Zeitgeist is still very much alive. While I agree with the argument of Matthijs Rooduijn that it hasn't led to many policy changes, proposed or implemented, that was never the core of my argument. I mainly claimed that the political and public discourse had become increasingly populist, with media and politicians pandering to an illusionary, homogeneous "the people" and criticizing an amoral "the elite" (even if it at times includes their own party). On top of that, populist parties have significantly increased their support since I wrote that article, both some of the established radical right parties (like FN and FPÖ) and some new radical left (e.g. Podemos and SYRIZA) and idiosyncratic populist parties (like the Five Star Movement).

POP: 7 Let's talk "European" for a moment. And Europe, in this historical juncture, means three things: migrants, terrorism, and economic crisis. Who is profiting more from this situation: right-wing populists against the migrants (PEGIDA, Alternative for Germany (AfD), Front National)? Left-wing populists against the Troika (SYRIZA, Podemos)? Or could it be the case that the only political actors considered able to cope with terrorism are the mainstream and established ones (Merkel, Hollande, Renzi)?

CM: I think it is too early to state unequivocally which group profits the most. It is clear that left populism has limited appeal. There are only a few truly successful cases; both new parties still have to prove their longevity. More established left populist parties like Die Linke in Germany, Sinn Féin in Ireland, and the Socialist Party in the Netherlands have hardly profited so far. Overall right-wing populist parties have profited a lot, in their various permutations, although the success is very unequal and some seem to suffer from government participation (e.g. Progress Party and Finns Party). The biggest winner, sadly, is the "non-vote," which is mostly ignored in analyses. Turnout is decreasing rapidly in many countries, not just in second-order elections. In the last Greek elections non-voters were the plurality and that country has compulsory voting!

POP: 8 What is the role of the media? Joseph Pulitzer claimed that "a cynical, mercenary, demagogic press will in time produce a people as base as itself." Do you think the media are giving an advantage to populist parties and creating cynical and disillusioned citizens?

CM: Sure, the transformation of the media landscape favors the populists, who provide the ammunition for the alarmist and sensationalist stories that commercial media thrive upon. Moreover, many populist parties have leaders who are particularly skillful at using the media, including social media. However, they are helped by the lack of mainstream alternatives. Mainstream parties have shed ideology for pragmatism and ideologues for pragmatists, who make for bad media stories. This is not a given, however, and non-populist parties and politicians can (re)gain the media spotlight, as happened with ANO in the Czech Republic and Cuidadanos in Spain.

POP: 9 Ten-million-dollar question. Do you think populism, both in the USA and Europe, is here to stay?

CM: Yes, in one shape or another. There are fundamental societal transformations underlying the rise of populism, including "cognitive mobilization" (Ronald Inglehart), ideological convergence of mainstream parties, the rise of undemocratic liberalism, and the transformation of the media landscape. These won't go away when the Great Recession is finally over.

Notes

1 This interview was first published on the website *POP – Political Observer on Populism* (30 May 2016).
2 See Cas Mudde, "The Populist Zeitgeist," *Government and Opposition*, Vol. 39, No. 4, 2004, pp. 541–563.

15 The far right has arrived ... and it could take Washington!

Donald Trump has brought far right politics into the mainstream of US politics. He is the first far right presidential candidate of one of the two major political parties in the US, at least since the end of the Second World War. This directly makes the US one of the Western democracies with the most popular far right politician.[1]

Last fall I taught my course "Far Right Politics in Western Democracies" at the University of Georgia. As usual, my students had little idea what the "far right" is and, as far as they associated it with any organizations, linked it to marginal groups like the Ku Klux Klan (KKK) or to historical phenomena like Adolf Hitler and National Socialism. Given their almost complete lack of knowledge of non-US politics, references to Marine Le Pen and the French National Front (FN) or Geert Wilders and the Dutch Party for Freedom (PVV) didn't help much, and neither did historical US examples like George Wallace or Pat Buchanan. In previous years students would leave the course with the idea that far right politics is mainly a European phenomenon. Not this time.

Donald Trump has brought far right politics into the mainstream of US politics. What Wallace and Buchanan were never able to achieve, despite gaining significant electoral and political influence, Trump has accomplished. He is the first far right presidential candidate of one of the two major political parties in the US, at least since the end of the Second World War. And, despite some half-hearted opposition by Ted Cruz, his candidacy was accepted and endorsed by much of the GOP leadership. This directly makes the US one of the Western democracies with the most popular far right politician – together with Austria (Norbert Hofer) and Hungary (Viktor Orbán).

Yesterday's acceptance speech created huge enthusiasm among the far right in the US. For example, former Klan leader David Duke, like Trump not a man known for his modesty, tweeted that he "couldn't have said it better" – I'm sure Geert Wilders felt the same. The speech was a combination of Alabama tolerance and New York nuance – incidentally, how ironic that the speech for the ultimate political outsider was written by a lifelong insider, Stephen Miller, a thirty-year-old with nine years' experience on Capitol Hill (working for radical right Alabama Senator Jeff Sessions, one of the first high-profile Trump supporters in the Republican Party). It had the apocalyptic fever of far right speeches, full of elite betrayal, alien threats, and authoritarian "solutions" – all covered in an onslaught of lies and half-truths.

Most striking about Trump's form of radical right politics is its combination of elitism and populism (see Chapters 10 and 13). Paradoxically, the country with the strongest populist tradition has a far right politician with a relatively weak populist discourse. Sure, he claimed to be "your champion in the White House" and pledged (in capitals in the original text): "I'M WITH YOU – THE AMERICAN PEOPLE." But, this seems mostly a way to attack Hillary Clinton, pitting his slogan "I'm with you" to her slogan "I'm with her." Much more importantly, he also stated, as he has done many times before, "Nobody knows the system better than me. Which is why I alone can fix it." In other words, The Donald is the unique savior rather than just one of the (common) people.

Most liberals believe that Trump cannot win the presidential election. His unfavorability numbers are simply too high. I used to think so too, but then again, I also thought that Trump could never win the Republican nomination and that the United Kingdom's "Brexit" from the European Union would not get a majority vote in the referendum. I no longer make predictions on Trump. In the old world he would have stood no chance, but this is a scared new world. A world in which established politicians no longer inspire but are instead met with popular disgust and distrust – no one more so than the presidential candidate for the Democratic Party, Hillary Clinton, whose unfavorability ratings are rivaling Trump's.

Note

1 This chapter was first published in the *Huffington Post* (22 July 2016).

16 The revenge of the losers of globalization?

Brexit, Trump and globalization

Received wisdom holds that the recent rise of populism in the West is the revenge of the so-called losers of globalization. But what is this "loser of globalization theory" and how useful is it to explain recent populist phenomena like Brexit and Trump?[1]

They seem to be everywhere these days, the so-called "losers of globalization," and their anger is allegedly transforming politics across the globe. From Brexit to the rise of Trump, globalization is the explanation and its losers are to blame. Some even extend the argument to the rise of Islamic fundamentalism and ISIS!

In a nutshell, the thesis holds that "globalization" has led to profound economic changes, which have transformed and divided societies. The ones who profit from these changes, mostly better educated and mobile (upper) middle classes that work in the service sector, are the "winners" of globalization, and support the mainstream parties that have implemented neoliberal policies. The ones who suffer because of these policies, mostly lower-educated men in the industrial sector, are the "losers" of globalization and support populist parties.

The "loser of globalization thesis" is quite simple, which explains its broad popularity. In fact, it has been popular for a long time, as it is merely the latest iteration of the decades-old modernization thesis, which has been used for many decades to explain the rise of nationalism in Europe in the 19th century. And since the rise of populist radical right parties in Europe started in the 1990s, the "losers of globalization thesis" has dominated both the academic and public debates.

The thesis is often also quite elitist, which explains its popularity among the better-educated part of the population (in terms of the theory: the winners of globalization). It is about "them," the uneducated masses, not "us," the educated elites. *They* cannot deal with the realities of a changing world and find solace in the simplistic solutions offered by populists – whereas *we* understand the complexities of the contemporary world and therefore support pro-globalization policies. This discourse was particularly dominant with regard to the Brexit referendum.

But for all the intellectual and personal comfort the "losers of globalization thesis" provides *us*, it is almost as stereotypical and simplistic as the populist discourse *we* abhor. First of all, in objective terms, there are not that many losers of globalization in most Western countries. Almost everyone has profited in some way. Moreover, as several people have pointed out for the case of the US, but hardly anyone for Europe, many of the real losers of globalization are not the white working class, but the non-white underclass, of African Americans in the US and immigrants (and their descendants) in Europe.

The thesis probably is more accurate when we look at *relative* rather than absolute deprivation, i.e. if we define the losers of globalization as those that *perceive* themselves to be losers. These are people who might have objectively profited from globalization, but who feel that they haven't profited *as much* as others. They will be actually correct: in the past decades a small minority (sometimes referred to as "the 1 percent") has profited disproportionally from the globalized economy. And, yet, populist radical right parties attract only a small part of these relative losers of modernization – even Brexit attracted "only" 52 percent of the people (just over half of "the 99 percent"!).

Another problem with the thesis is its theoretical underdevelopment. Why would the losers of globalization vote for Donald Trump, who doesn't fundamentally oppose neoliberal globalization, instead of Bernie Sanders, who does (as least much more fundamentally)? If this truly was about a fairer redistribution of wealth and bringing back well-paying working-class jobs to Europe and the US, the populist left is a much more authentic voice of the losers of modernization than the populist right. And yet, even after almost a decade of the Great Recession, the populist left is quite marginal, outside Greece and Spain, while the populist right has reached unprecedented heights in many more countries.

The past years have taught us that a predominantly socio-economic anti-globalization discourse is only successful in countries that experience severe economic crises and/or economic inequality – such as Greece, Venezuela, and the United States. In most countries it is the *socio-cultural translation of socio-economic grievances* that fuels the rise of the populist right. While people might be frustrated or worried about their socio-economic situation, it is the link to socio-cultural threats – from China to the Middle East and from (Muslim) immigrants to "femiNazis" – that mobilizes them to *voice* support for a radical alternative – rather than *exit* with a non-vote or express *loyalty* by voting for the mainstream alternative.

60 *The revenge of the losers of globalization?*

In short, support for right populist politics is not a matter of *either* economic woes *or* xenophobia; it is both, wrapped up in a boiling hot blanket of anti-establishment anger. This also means that populist right politics will remain viable after the Great Recession has ended, as we can see in the largely post-recession US. Hence, simply providing a fairer redistributive socio-economic policy is not going to get rid of populist right politics – although it will undoubtedly limit its success. First of all, part of the population is Islamophobic and even racist, irrespective of their socio-economic position. They might never support liberal democratic politics within a multi-ethnic society. Second, many others are deeply suspicious of the political establishment, which includes academics and journalists, and will have to be convinced, over a long period of time, that these new policies are indeed profitable for them and that "others" are not profiting (much) more. That is the real challenge for the future: to create a politics that is more fair and inclusive to all, both the (mostly white) *relative* and the (mostly non-white) *absolute* "losers of globalization."

Note

1 This chapter was first published in the *Huffington Post* (9 August 2016).

17   Stop using the term "alt-right"!

The media star of the 2016 presidential election is the "alt-right," the new "evil darling" of the media. Article after article proclaims the novelty of the so-called "alt-right," even though the group and the term remain covered in vagueness.[1]

Ten years ago I attended a conference in an upscale national chain hotel in a small town in Virginia, just outside Dulles International Airport. Even though we were all wearing badges with our name and affiliation or place, it wasn't one of the usual academic conferences I frequent. The stands were selling books that claim to prove the intellectual superiority of the "white race," while in the whirlpool a woman and two men were discussing which town had the best Ku Klux Klan (KKK) chapter for her children. In the plenary room a broad variety of speakers were lambasting "race traitors" and entertaining their audience of a couple hundred people with more and less subtle anti-Semitic and racist "jokes."

It was the annual conference of *American Renaissance*, a magazine that, according to its website, "promotes a variety of white racial positions." Its leader, Jared Taylor, has long tried to mainstream racist ideology in the United States. Although Taylor would stay away from addressing "the Jewish issue" himself, and even reach out to Jewish conservatives, he had no problem with collaborating with vicious anti-Semites like David Duke, a former KKK Grand Wizard, or Don Black, founder of the main neo-Nazi internet forum, Stormfront. In fact, the most surreal experience occurred when Duke referred to "people of Lithuanian descent" in his speech – one of many not so subtle code words anti-Semites use to refer to Jews. An older man in the audience stood up, identified himself as Jewish, shouted that Duke was an anti-Semite, and stormed out of the room. How he could have sat through the previous two days of anti-Semitism and racism without understanding the premise of the conference was beyond me.

62 *Stop using the term "alt-right"!*

Jared Taylor and *American Renaissance* are among the main representatives of what many in the media have started to call the "alt-right." The term itself was never used by Taylor, or most of the other people now linked to the term. It was allegedly coined by Richard B. Spencer, who founded the website Alternative Right in 2010. In many ways Spencer is a younger version of Taylor: well educated, in tune with modern technology, and determined to bridge the gap between conservatives and "racial realists" (i.e. closet white supremacists). He is president of a think tank with the perfectly respectable name National Policy Institute (NPI), which attends and organizes conferences, including the more mainstream Conservative Political Action Conference (CPAC).

Both Spencer and the term "alt-right" were marginal within the US right, and unknown to the US public, until the rise of Donald Trump. And it is actually not so much Trump but the mainstream media that has made them into recognizable names. In a misguided strategy of guilt-by-association, as if Trump's own words don't speak for themselves, Duke, Spencer and Taylor have been interviewed and mainstreamed by leading media outlets, expressing their support for Trump, arguing that he says what they have been saying all along. This has rejuvenated these moribund organizations and undoubtedly strengthened their appeal and support, at least in the social media. Similarly, the term "alt-right" is now used as if it has any clear meaning.

But unlike terms like conservatism and radical right, "alt-right" has no clear definition or philosophical foundations. It is also not new. Groups like *American Renaissance* have been around for decades. The term "alt-right" is nothing more than a clever marketing tool by a white supremacist activist, who knows that his ideology is considered unacceptable in today's society. Hence, he came up with a term that sounds acceptable to the conservative mainstream. For years it had little to no effect until uncritical and uninformed journalists did what he never could: mainstream his term.

Tellingly, with a few notable exceptions, most of the main individuals and organizations that are described as part of the "alt-right" by the media do not self-identify as such. While they use all kind of other neologisms, like "racial realist" and "white nationalist," they are, and always have been, white supremacists! They are racists (not "racialists") who believe in the existence of races and in the superiority of the "white race." As anyone with the most basic understanding of US history knows, there is *nothing* new about this!

Note

1 This chapter was first published in the *Huffington Post* (25 August 2016).

18 Why is American political science blind on the right eye?

Despite the fact that thousands of political scientists study US politics, US political science has been caught off-guard by every single right-wing phenomenon of the past decades. Whether it was neoconservatism or Trumpism, the Tea Party or the so-called "alt-right," US political science didn't see it coming and devoted precious few resources to understanding it. What explains this continuing blind spot?[1]

This Thursday thousands of (mostly) American political scientists will descend upon Philadelphia for the annual meeting of the American Political Science Association (APSA). A plurality, if not a majority, of those scholars work exclusively on American politics. While the rise of Donald Trump will undoubtedly be heatedly debated in the hallways and panels, only a few papers are actually devoted to explaining the most important development in US politics this year. This (again) begs the question: why is American political science blind on the right eye?

Three of the most discussed political phenomena in American politics this century are of a (radical) right nature: neoconservatism, the Tea Party, and Trump(ism). All three developments took US political scientists by surprise, and the discipline is still struggling with finding a convincing and comprehensive explanation for them – I could also include far right terrorism, which is considered to be "the most severe threat of political violence" by US law enforcement agencies, but is hardly studied by US political scientists. To be fair, while the situation is not much better with regard to the radical left, Bernie Sanders, Black Lives Matter and particularly Occupy Wall Street have drawn much more interest from American political scientists (while they are much less relevant to American politics).

In 2008 I set out to write a review article on the political science literature on neoconservatism for the *Journal of Politics*. It was a response to the received wisdom that "neoconservatives" had dominated the Bush administration, most notably in pushing through the Iraq invasion. But while this alleged neoconservative influence was noted in many academic accounts, I was unable to find any political science study of neoconservatism. In the end, I had to broaden my review article to also include conservatism in general and rely almost exclusively on books by conservative activists and historians.[2] Even today the main book on the US neoconservative movement is written by a French bureaucrat, and previous think tanker, Justin Vaïsse, and was translated from French![3]

Similarly, the rise of the Tea Party movement took the discipline by total surprise. This was even more surprising as the previous major right-wing social movement, the Christian Right, had been the subject of study of American political scientists, including some prominent scholars like Mark J. Rozell and Clyde Wilcox. And while the Tea Party movement did inspire some original scholarship, including from prominent scholars like Theda Skocpol (see Chapter 33), its lessons seem to have been quickly forgotten, as they (and the Tea Party movement in general) hardly feature in the discussion of the third right-wing surprise: the rise of Donald Trump.

The rise of Donald Trump took almost everyone by surprise, and I was no exception. That said, I was more surprised by the rise of Trump than of Trumpism. After all, radical right politics have a long history in the US, dating at least back to the nativist Know Nothings of the mid-19th century (see Chapter 2), and recent developments, including the Tea Party and the right turn of the GOP, had awakened fires that the vast network of right-wing media were happy to stoke with more fuel. But as journalists looked for political scientists to explain the "Trump phenomenon" they found few scholars of the US radical right and instead turned to those of the European radical right.

Only in the past months, a year after Trump declared that he was running for president and more than half a year after he started to dominate the GOP primaries, are we seeing an increasingly lively debate on the reasons for Trump's success among American political scientists – importantly, this debate is largely taking place in the media. Still, little of the research is rooted in the study of the US radical right. Most is a reflection of well-established fields of study, i.e. on authoritarian personalities, "losers of modernization" (see Chapter 16), or racial prejudice.

How can scholars of American politics time and again be taken by surprise by the rise of radical right movements? Moreover, why do scholars of American politics ignore the radical right, while those of European politics obsess over it? There is no doubt that the specific two-party system in the US plays a role – there are no clear radical right parties like the French National Front (FN) or the Dutch Party for Freedom (PVV) to be studied. Still, even the United Kingdom, which also has a two-party system, has some (more or less) radical right parties, like the British National Party (BNP) and the UK Independence Party (UKIP), that contest elections and have been studied in detail. But this is only part of the story.

A more important, and troubling, part of the problem is inherent in US political science in general, and the study of American politics in particular. Over the past decades US political science has become more and more (meta)theoretically and methodologically homogeneous, particularly at the more prestigious top research universities, which train a majority of the political scientists at other research-intensive universities.

At the (meta)theoretical level Rational Choice Theory (RCT) dominates much of the research, which (very simply stated) assumes that all politics is driven by individuals who are exclusively driven by economic self-interest. In this highly sanitized and simplistic world, ideologies and identities are secondary at best, and irrelevant at worst. In fact, politics as a whole is often reduced to a "logical" consequence of economic and sociological developments – in more academic terms, the focus is exclusively on the demand side of (electoral) politics, while the supply side is ignored.

At the methodological level, statistical methods are the gold standard, and the more advanced the method, the better the research. This has made the study of American politics, in particular, extremely data-driven. But data suitable for complex statistical analyses have at least two fundamental problems. First, they simplify the complex social and political world – think about one of the most-used datasets of political regimes, by Freedom House, which has just three categories: free, partly free, and not free. Second, most elaborate datasets are only developed *after* a phenomenon becomes politically relevant, and hence significant funding can be secured. This means that quantitative political scientists are often many years behind the curve.

Finally, the study of American politics is significantly weakened by a very strong parochialism. While American politics is part of comparative politics in all other countries, it is almost completely separated from it in the US. Not only do many scholars of American politics study the US in isolation – yet consider their findings relevant to the whole world – but they don't even draw upon scholarship of similar phenomena in other countries.

Perhaps the rise of Trump will finally lead to some critical introspection and, wishful thinking, structural change within US political science in general, and the study of American politics in particular. It has already led scholars to draw upon examples of European politics, most notably Silvio Berlusconi and Marine Le Pen (see Chapter 9). It has also led to critical reflections on dominant theses within the study of American politics, such as the crucial importance of money (Citizens United) or "the party" in US politics (see Chapter 28). Still, without a more methodologically and theoretically pluralistic approach, as well as a more comparative perspective, US political science will continue to struggle to anticipate and explain key developments in US politics.

Notes

1 This chapter was first published in the *Huffington Post* (29 August 2016).
2 See Cas Mudde, "The Rise (and Fall) of American Conservatism," *Journal of Politics*, Vol. 72, No. 2, 2010, pp. 588–594.
3 I am referring to Justin Vaïsse, *Neoconservatism: The Biography of a Movement* (Cambridge, MA: Harvard University Press, 2011).

19 Did Trump really hijack the GOP?

Now that Donald Trump has secured the presidential nomination for the Republican Party, conservatives (and a surprising number of liberals) keep claiming that Trump is not really a Republican and "hijacked" the Grand Old Party (GOP). But did he really?[1]

Ever since Donald Trump became the presidential candidate for the Republican Party, the party establishment has claimed that the real estate mogul-turned reality TV star-turned politician has "hijacked" the Grand Old Party (GOP). Their argument is that the GOP stands for very different values than Trump and Trumpism. Some critics have countered that this might hold true for the party establishment, but not, or less so, for the party supporters, let alone those who vote in the party's primaries.

When one looks at the 2016 Republican platform, which is supposed to be the official position of the whole party, it does seem that the GOP and Trump(ism) have little in common. The platform is a fairly traditional GOP document, defending US exceptionalism, the free market, the traditional family, and other Republican classics. It mainly reflects Trumpist positions in its almost obsessive attacks on President Obama and its harsh tone on "illegal immigration" and "illegal immigrants." That said, both are popular tropes within the GOP and Trump is hardly the only leading Republican to espouse them repeatedly. More importantly, the platform is largely a symbolic document, traditionally ignored by the presidential candidate as well as most of the party's national, regional, and local representatives.

If Trump has truly *hijacked* the GOP, it would mean that the party did not already have many prominent radical right representatives before his ascendance to party prominence. This is true if we focus exclusively on the most visible party leaders, like (toothless) party leader Reince Priebus, Senate minority leader Mitch McConnell, House majority leader Kevin McCarthy or House Speaker Paul Ryan. But at least a minority of its members of Congress openly hold radical right positions, such as Louie Gohmert (Texas) and Steve King (Iowa) in the House of Representatives, as well as Ted Cruz (Texas) and Jeff Sessions (Alabama) in the Senate. Gohmert and King regularly meet up with European radical right leaders, including AfD leader Frauke Petry and PVV leader Geert Wilders.

Moreover, radical right politics – inspired by authoritarianism, nativism and populism – run rampant at the state and local levels, among governors and legislators alike. For example, it is almost exclusively among GOP-controlled states that strict anti-immigration and "anti-Sharia" legislation has been introduced. And the vast majority of Republican governors refused to accept Syrian refugees into their states, on the unfounded allegation that they would include terrorists. It is also at the state and local levels that the links between the GOP and established radical right groups, like the John Birch Society (JBS) and various white supremacist groups – misguidedly referred to as "alt-right" in many media – are often much more open.

So, while Trump is perhaps not very representative of the GOP at the federal level, this is not true at the state (or local) level – particularly in the American "heartland" between the two coasts. And if we look at the level of the party supporter, Trump is in many ways a much more accurate *representative* of the GOP electorate than party establishment politicians like Mitch McConnell and failed presidential candidate Jeb Bush.

Poll after poll has shown that a plurality if not an outright majority of GOP supporters, not just those who support Trump, hold authoritarian, nativist, and even racist attitudes. For example, a 2012 poll, well before the rise of Trump, found that 79 percent of Republicans expressed (explicit) racial prejudice about African Americans; to be fair, the differences between white Republicans and white Democrats towards African Americans are not so large, but the Republicans have by now an almost completely white electorate, while Democrats have a much more diverse support base. On other minorities the numbers are not much better: in a 2015 poll 59 percent of Republicans believed that immigrants have a negative impact on US society, while in a 2014 poll clear majorities of Republicans held negative views on both Arab Americans and Muslim Americans.

Similarly, conspiracy theories about issues like global warming and refugees as well as political opponents like President Obama and Hillary Clinton find broad support among the broader GOP electorate. For example, a staggering 81 percent of Republicans think it is (definitely or possibly) true that Hillary Clinton "knew the US Embassy in

Benghazi was going to be attacked and did nothing to protect it," 54 percent think the same about the statement "global warming is a myth concocted by scientists," and 53 percent believe that Obama was not born in the US.

This is not surprising, as GOP politicians have enthusiastically expressed versions of these conspiracy theories and prejudices for years. In fact, both the 2012 and 2016 GOP primaries were full of presidential hopefuls espousing nativist sentiments. This year all major candidates proposed to limit the rights of minorities such as gays and Muslims. In fact, the three last-standing candidates in the primaries (Cruz, Rubio and Trump) *all* called for increased monitoring of "Muslim communities" in sharp opposition to religious freedom and, obviously, the First Amendment. And Cruz, the second most popular Republican in the primaries, is one of the most prominent supporters of many of the most popular far right conspiracy theories in the US (see also Chapter 11).

In short, there is little evidence for the thesis that Donald Trump is a far right outsider who has infiltrated a mainstream right-wing party, as the establishment is desperately trying to tell you and most mainstream media continue to confirm. If Trump really has hijacked the GOP, he hijacked it from its leaders, not from its supporters. Moreover, given that almost all major leaders have by now endorsed Trump as their party's presidential candidate, it seems that the GOP leadership is suffering from Stockholm Syndrome.

Note

1 This chapter was first published in *HOPE not hate Magazine* (US Election Special, October 2016).

20 The latest Trump (and GOP and media) fiasco in nine points

The tape of the "locker room conversation" of Donald Trump and Today Show host Billy Bush, in which the Republican presidential nominee bragged about grabbing women "by the pussy," has caused a storm of public outrage by journalists and politicians, but has also yet again showed the many ways in which the media are failing us in covering the 2016 presidential election.[1]

The candidacy of Donald Trump has led to many "firsts" in US politics. Among them is also the first time that both the male and female genitals have become topics of official campaign discussion. The latest – although probably by the time I finish this blog post there is already a newer – Trump scandal is about a secret tape in which he brags about grabbing women "by the pussy," which was made during a locker room conversation with *Today Show* host Billy Bush – who, for inexplicable reasons, is still not fired by NBC.

As so often in this presidential campaign, the media are by and large failing us, breaking news (although often by being handed the information rather than by investigative journalism), sensationalizing it, and then not following up on it with critical analysis of what is really happening. So, here is my quick analysis, summarized in nine points.

20.1 This is about sexual assault, not about sexist remarks!

The story was broken by *Washington Post* reporter David Fahrenthold in a piece entitled "Trump recorded having extremely lewd conversation about women in 2005." But the essence of the piece was not "lewd conversation," it was straight-up sexual assault and (probably) rape. In the conversation with Bush, in a locker room, Trump bragged about kissing women without consent and grabbing them between their legs! *That* was the story: sexual assault, not sexist remarks!

20.2 If it were about sexist remarks, there would be no reason for the "outcry"

In fact, if the story were truly "just" about sexist remarks, as also almost all GOP politicians (pro- or anti-Trump) emphasized, there would have been absolutely zero news value in it. You hardly have to go to 2005 to find sexist remarks by Donald Trump. He makes them constantly, and not just in the locker room either – just remember the "blood coming out of her wherever" remark about Fox News anchor Megyn Kelly.

20.3 If this is your "locker room banter," you should change your gym!

Donald Trump himself lightly dismissed the remarks as "locker room banter," a phrase that was eagerly adopted by GOP and Trump surrogates in a (not unsuccessful) attempt to distract discussion from their candidate – as was the predictable attack on Bill Clinton, which Fox News presenter and Trump booster Sean Hanley ran away with. Again, the issue here is sexual assault (i.e. criminal behavior), and not sexist remarks (i.e. legal speech). But if you do want to go there, this is *not* normal locker room banter! I have never heard anyone talk openly and proudly about sexually assaulting a woman in any locker room – and I am certain that if I had, I wouldn't have laughed like a sexually frustrated teenager (as the still-not-fired Billy Bush did). Still, if this truly is what your locker room banter is like, I advise you to immediately change your gym!

20.4 GOP "outcry" is about the messenger, not the message

Since the news broke, most high-ranking Republicans have denounced Trump's remarks – while completely ignoring his claimed behavior – although very few have openly renounced their endorsement of him. Even the ones that are, behind closed doors, trying to get Trump to step back, are clearly much more upset about the messenger than about the message. They are worried that Trump is too damaged to win the election. Hence, they are looking for someone else who can more successfully promote roughly the same message.

20.5 This is not about your daughters and wives, it is about *all* women!

Another striking aspect about the response of many Republicans is their personalization of the remarks. They also seem mainly concerned about their own female relatives, endlessly referring to their daughters and wives, rather than about women in general. In short, we don't want you to talk about *our women* like that – although Ted Cruz seems perfectly fine with working for a man who has made numerous sexist and degrading remarks about his own wife.

20.6 Don't insult (our) white women but feel free to attack all non-white minorities

Similarly, it is very telling that (only) these remarks were unacceptable to so many Republicans, who have been silent or tolerant towards Trump's often even worse remarks about other groups. He has likened Muslims to snakes and terrorists, and Mexicans to criminals and, oh the irony, rapists. And yet, it was only when he spoke badly about (our) *white* women that these Republicans were "appalled" and started to doubt their support for Trump.

20.7 Republicans will probably lose with Trump, but certainly without him

The fact that high-ranking Republicans are wasting their time even considering alternatives for Trump – like running-mate Mike Pence and failed 2012 candidate Mitt Romney – shows how delusional they are about both Trump and the Trump phenomenon. There is little to no realistic chance that Trump will gracefully bow out of the race – even if he were to withdraw, and that is an enormous *if*, he would undoubtedly make it look like it was a conspiracy and he was the victim of the GOP elite. Any removal of Trump, however spun by the Republican establishment, will ensure that a sizeable part of the real Trump electorate will not vote in next month's elections. They already now hate the GOP establishment almost as much as they hate Hillary Clinton. In short, while the Republicans will *probably* lose with Trump, they will *certainly* lose without him!

20.8 It is crucial for US democracy that Trump is defeated by the electorate, not by the GOP establishment

The backroom deals that are going on within Republican circles are not just problematic for the GOP, they constitute a serious threat to liberal democracy in the country. It will "prove" to the hardcore Trump supporters that they have no voice in the current democratic system and that when they finally play by the rules, the establishment intervenes. This will undoubtedly lead to many Trump supporters to (again) turn their back on the democratic system and the electoral process. This is problematic from a broader democratic point of view, which holds that democracy functions best when as many people as possible participate. But it is also worrying because it concerns a specific part of the population that is particularly susceptible to conspiracy theories and is heavily armed.

20.9 The only hope for the GOP is a Goldwater moment

Those who truly want to reform the Grand Old Party, and take it back from the radical right of both Trump and Cruz (as well as many others), should let Trump contest the election on his own accord and wait for a Goldwater moment, i.e. a massive electoral defeat that will allow political space for a fundamental reform of the party. Only if Trumpism is electorally defeated will leading Republicans have the opportunity and will (courage would be too strong a term) to pull the party back in a liberal democratic direction, and (re)build the heavily damaged relationships with the groups that will define the majority of the electorate in the years to come, most notably Hispanics and women.

Note

1 This chapter was first published in the *Huffington Post* (8 October 2016).

21 Brexit, Trump, and five (wrong) lessons about "the populist challenge"

Brexit and Trump have made populism the buzzword of the international media. Everything is populism and everyone is a populism expert. But while populism is an important concept to understand contemporary politics in many democracies around the world, it tells only part of the story.[1]

If populism wasn't already the political buzzword of the 21st century before the Brexit vote in the United Kingdom (UK) and the rise of Trump in the United States (US), it surely is now. Media stories about populism have been proliferating at an exponential rate, as have populism "experts." Everything is populism and everyone is a populism expert.

But while populism is an important concept to understand contemporary politics in many democracies around the world, it tells only part of the story. This is because populism is a so-called "thin" ideology, which is almost always combined with one or more other ideologies when political actors are successful. Moreover, the success of populist actors, like all political actors, is dependent upon the cultural and political system they operate in (and rarely have helped shape before they became successful).

I'll illustrate both points on the basis of two of the most striking political developments in Western democracies of this year, the Brexit vote and the rise of Trump, which have become the prime examples of successful populism in much recent reporting.

21.1 Brexit and Trump are at least as much about nativism as about populism

There is no doubt that populism – *a thin-centered ideology that considers society to be ultimately separated into two homogeneous and antagonistic groups, "the pure people" and "the corrupt elite," and which argues that politics should be an expression of the* volonté générale *(general will) of the people* – has played an important role in the success of both Brexit and Trump. Both campaigns attack(ed) "the corrupt elite" for stifling "the people" and betraying the "general will" (or "silent majority") – although Trump himself is more elitist than populist (see Chapter 10). But that is only part of the story.

At the core of the Brexit campaign was nationalism, i.e. the idea that the British people should be sovereign in their own country. Nationalism was what combined all forces within the Leave camp, from establishment Tories (members of the Conservative Party) to anti-establishment Kippers (members of the United Kingdom Independence Party, UKIP). On top of that, xenophobia towards both Eastern Europeans and non-Europeans (mostly Muslims) was instrumental in pushing the Leave camp to a majority. In other words, nativism – i.e. xenophobic nationalism – was at least as important as populism.

This is even more the case for Trump, who emerged victorious in the primaries within a deep field of populists. Particularly at his early rallies audiences would be near-comatose as Trump rattled off his own achievements (e.g. selling condos to *the* Chinese), get only slightly excited when he attacked the political establishment ("*the* Washington elite"), but get really rowdy when he went after *the* Mexicans and *the* Muslims. And although nativism is certainly not limited to Trump within the Republican Party, it has been the core of his campaign from the beginning – in fact, even before that, as he entered the national political debate as the most ferocious voice of Birtherism.[2]

21.2 Brexit support was only partly populist radical right

While Brexit (and Trump) was not just about populism, but a specific form of *right-wing* populism (which I call the populist radical right),[3] it was also a highly complex phenomenon, which has some similarities to, but also important differences from, populist radical right *parties* in Europe. Crucially, the UK referendum followed a majoritarian logic, in which voters only had two options: Leave or Remain.

This limited choice brought together broad alliances of people who were pro- and anti-European Union (EU) membership. For example, the Leave camp included civic nationalists, open to multiculturalism but hostile to limited sovereignty; nativists, against both immigrants and the EU; neoliberals, who believe the EU stifles the free market with its bureaucracy and social legislation; as well as a smaller group of radical left voters, who fundamentally oppose the EU as a neoliberal project.

21.3 Trump voters versus Trump supporters

The electorate that will vote for Trump on November 8 is not the same as the one that has voted for him in the primaries. It will not only be much bigger, but it will also be much more diverse. The *real* Trump electorate, i.e. the people who truly *support* Trump – not just over Hillary Clinton but over anyone, including other Republicans – lies somewhere in between the Trump electorate in the Republican primaries and his electorate in the presidential election – though much closer to the former than the latter.

Only a small and selective portion of Republicans vote in the primaries, irrespective of the candidates. But in the presidential election, many people will vote for Trump out of party loyalty or out of disdain for Hillary Clinton (or because of both). They would prefer to vote for a non-radical right Republican candidate, such as John Kasich or Marco Rubio, but they don't have that choice. Voters in Europe do, because they can vote for a conservative or a neoliberal party without "wasting" their vote – as most countries use some form of proportional representation that also gives parliamentary representation to smaller parties.

The exception is the two-round presidential election that countries like Austria (next month) and France (next year) use. Here the first round works a little similarly to the primary process in the US, i.e. selecting the most popular left and right candidates for the run-off. Hence, the primaries electorate of Trump is more similar to the first-round electorates of Norbert Hofer and Marine Le Pen, while his presidential electorate is more similar to the second-round electorates of Hofer and, though to a lesser extent, Le Pen. The latter combine the core populist radical right support – i.e. which populist radical right parties would attract in elections with a proportional system – with a more diverse electorate that simply votes against the other candidate.

21.4 Brexit and Trump are about the mainstreaming of populist radical right politics (or the radicalization of mainstream politics)

Rather than seeing the Brexit and Trump votes as indicators of the support of the populist radical right, they should be viewed as indicators of the increasing mainstreaming of populist radical right politics and politicians. For at least two decades populist radical right *politics* have been almost exclusive to populist radical right *parties* – while mainstream parties did at times adopt some of the rhetoric, they rarely fundamentally changed their ideologies or policies. Populist radical right parties and politicians were mostly shunned or accepted under specific circumstances – for example, the Austrian Freedom Party (FPÖ) could only enter the government without its (then) leader, Jörg Haider. Although this is still somewhat the case in the Brexit and Trump examples – for example, some Conservatives within the Leave campaign kept UKIP leader Nigel Farage at a distance, while many within the GOP establishment do not openly support Trump (but will vote for him) – the merger between mainstream and radical right is intensifying.

This merger of mainstream right and populist radical right is almost complete in some Eastern-Central European countries, like Hungary and Poland, where formerly conservative politicians now openly voice populist radical right ideas while remaining comfortably within their mainstream right political groups within the EU. But it is also affecting several established right-wing parties and politicians in Western Europe, as can be seen in the recent statements by former French president, and 2017 presidential hopeful, Nicolas Sarkozy, as well as by various leaders of the Christian Social Union (CSU) in Germany and the Conservative Party in the UK.

21.5 The real lesson is to look beyond populism and the usual suspects

In short, both populism and the usual populist suspects show only part of the current illiberal challenge to liberal democracy. There is a reason why radical right populists are much more successful than left-wing populists and that reason is nativism! Consequently, (radical right) populist actors will not disappear once the economic crisis is finally over, or even when the recent economic inequality has been undone – as several new populist experts are claiming.

At least as important, populist radical right politics is no longer tied only to the usual suspects, i.e. traditional populist radical right parties. Whether Sarkozy or Le Pen wins the 2017 presidential elections is at this point almost irrelevant. The almost certain implosion of UKIP will at best soften the increasingly authoritarian, nativist, and populist policies of the Tory government. And the predicted defeat of Trump will not mean the end of Trumpism within the GOP. That is the real challenge of liberal democrats going forward, i.e. the radicalization of the mainstream right. And as long as we equate populist radical right politics with (only) populist radical right parties, liberal democrats will fail to meet this challenge!

Notes

1 This chapter was first published in the *Huffington Post* (4 November 2016).
2 Birtherism is the unfounded accusation that President Barack Obama was not born in the United States. It became so popular in right-wing circles that Obama released his birth certificate, which showed that he was indeed born in Hawaii.
3 See Cas Mudde, *Populist Radical Right Parties in Europe* (New York: Cambridge University Press, 2007).

22 Keeping it real in Trump's America

The election of Donald Trump to president of the United States took many people by surprise. After months of highly polarized campaigning, it is important to take a step back, and rationally and realistically assess the potential threat to liberal democracy that Trump presents.[1]

Like many of my friends I am trying to come to terms with the reality of a Trump presidency, working through my own emotions and thoughts, while simultaneously consulting and being consulted by others. As an educator, parent, and public intellectual I have an obligation to provide an accurate assessment of the possible future, which neither ignores nor exaggerates the dangers. After all, we (educators, parents, and public intellectuals) are in a privileged position and should be aware of the power of our voice.

I am the father of a three-year-old son, who is fortunately too young to understand the ramifications of the recent elections. In fact, yesterday it was *his* oblivion that provided me and my wife with calm and strength, rather than the other way around. But I have many colleagues and friends who had to comfort their older children and adolescents, who were angry, sad, and sometimes terrified about their future and that of their friends. One colleague's child asked whether her Hispanic friend from elementary school would be deported. Another friend's son was terrified because Trump, the man his parents had castigated for months, is now going to be his president. In most cases the emotions of the children are primarily the result of the information about Trump and a Trump presidency they receive from their parents.

Many of my colleagues also wrote heart-breaking stories about students crying in class, looking for guidance. Many diverted from the scheduled topic of the day to discuss the elections and their possible ramifications for the US and the world – ranging from pure emotional therapy sessions to more academic discussions. It is important to reach out to your students, and be responsive when they reach out to you – particularly for educators who teach on topics related to (American) politics. We have a moral and professional responsibility to help them make sense of the world. But we should do this in an inclusive and informed way: the classroom should be a space for all opinions, including those of Trump voters, as long as they are expressed respectfully. I admit that this is not always possible – take, for example, the sincere expression of Islamophobic views in a classroom with Muslim students – but it is the role of the educator to help facilitate the dialogue and ensure it is based on credible facts, while allowing for different interpretations and evaluations of those facts.

Like many others, I was asked by journalists to comment on the election and speculate about the consequences of a Trump presidency. I have spoken mostly about the possible effects on the success of far right parties in Europe, my main expertise, and have been cautious not to overstate the effects. Given the fact that Trump has held virtually every position on almost every issue in the past years, has no administrative experience, and will probably be surrounded by mainly inexperienced people – with some exceptions, like former New York Mayor Rudy Giuliani and former House Speaker Newt Gingrich – it is irresponsible to claim to know the future beyond some broader, fairly standard right-wing, points.

Suggested similarities to Weimar Germany and fascist regimes are in most cases not just fundamentally flawed but also disingenuous and irresponsible. Weimar Germany had been democratic for a mere 15 years when Adolf Hitler came to power – the vast majority of the German elites and the masses at that time didn't believe in democracy and the mostly new political institutions were largely untested and weak. Whatever the problems of US democracy, and there are many more than are generally acknowledged, the system has been functioning for centuries and has withstood various tests (think, for example, of the Civil War and Watergate). The democratic system has protected the rights of most white citizens for centuries and the rights of most minority citizens for at least many decades. Both the US elites and masses overwhelmingly support democracy and the US democratic system. Moreover, while there are worrying aspects of Trump and his campaign, which are indeed reminiscent of *aspects* of fascism (e.g. nativism, racism, and an exceptionally high tolerance for violence), he lacks the ideological coherence and organizational structure of the fascist movements of the 1930s.

But even if some people truly believe that there are fundamental similarities between Trump and Weimar Germany, then I am puzzled why they are openly tweeting and writing about the dawning fascist

Trump regime. Particularly given their historic insight, knowing what fascist regimes are capable of, are these people truly so heroic that they are willing to face almost certain imprisonment if not outright death in Trump's America? If they really think that we are facing a fundamental threat to democracy and life, why don't they take their families into safety and move abroad?

I assume they don't do this because deep down they know full well that Trump isn't a fascist and the US isn't Weimar Germany. They can distinguish between their personal hyperbole and political reality. They know that things could get bad, although particularly for certain minorities (notably non-whites), but the basic institutions of US liberal democracy will survive and continue to protect them. Unfortunately, many people within their audiences do not know this and will actually internalize that frightening scenario. Looking to them for guidance, and respecting them as experts on the topic, they will truly believe that stormtroopers will roam the streets soon and concentration camps are just around the corner. This fear-mongering is ideological grand-standing at the expense of the weakest people, exactly what they (rightly) accuse Trump of!

This is not to argue that we should not emphasize the threats to *liberal* democracy that are inherent in the nativism and authoritarianism of Trump and his campaign, particularly to minority rights and the rule of law. But more than anything we should empower our audiences to defend liberal democracy rather than frighten them into submitting to alleged fascism. After all, only heroes stand up to a fascist regime and history has taught us that there are very few true heroes. Empowered citizens can help *protect* minority rights and rule of law, when indeed challenged, and can campaign to weaken the grip of Trump and the radical right wing of the Republican Party by taking back the Senate in 2018 and making Trump a one-term president in 2020.

Note

1 This chapter was first published in the *Huffington Post* (10 November 2016).

23 The far right in a Trump world

Europe's far right parties were among the most important and vocal supporters of Donald Trump during the election. What does his victory mean for the popular support and political influence of the European far right?[1]

The surprise victory of Donald Trump is a gift from right-wing heaven for the far right around the globe. Even more than providing "a friend in the White House," which will remain to be seen, it gives them a narrative of hope and success. After all, no one believed it was possible for Trump to seal the Republican nomination, let alone win the presidential election. If Trump can do it, out of the blue, without a solid ground game and in a majoritarian system, then surely Marine Le Pen can do it, supported by a four-decade old, well-organized political party. Moreover, even if the polls say she doesn't stand a chance in the second round of the French presidential elections, which she is almost certain to qualify for, weren't the polls saying the same of Trump (and Brexit)?

As everyone was expecting the first directly elected far right president of the postwar era to emerge in Austria, the country that gave us Adolf Hitler, it was in the United States, key to defeating Hitler, and with no history of significant electoral success for far right parties or politicians, that the increasingly inevitable happened. He is probably going to be joined by Norbert Hofer next month, as Austrians hold a re-run of their canceled presidential elections, which Hofer lost by the tiniest margin. But this is not the start of an explosion of far right presidents, if only because few European countries have directly elected presidents. Even Marine Le Pen, the most powerful far right politician in Europe, will almost certainly fail in the run-off, as center-left and center-right voters coalesce around whoever the mainstream candidate will be.

But far right parties will continue to win votes and seats, particularly in those countries where they have been more or less powerful forces for some time. They will become more accepted by the political mainstream, which has already been shifting significantly to the right in the wake of the so-called refugee crisis. And as mainstream politicians increasingly work harmoniously together with non-traditional far right politicians like Hungarian Premier Viktor Orbán and US President Trump, how will they be able to continue to justify the exclusion of domestic far right politicians like Le Pen and Geert Wilders – especially if those politicians, and their programs, will be openly endorsed by Orbán and Trump.

So does this mean that we are now facing a "Populist International," as some commentators have recently argued, a Putin-Trump axis with satellites in most European capitals? Not really. While far right leaders throughout Europe were among the first to congratulate President Trump, they were mostly celebrating the victory rather than the man himself. An exception was Nigel Farage, who shamelessly doubled down on his application to become US ambassador to Brussels. But Farage is also the only European far right leader who actually has a personal relationship with Trump, whom he allegedly coached for the debates with Hillary Clinton.

Most European far right leaders have a similar personal relationship with Trump as they have with Russian President Vladimir Putin – i.e. none. They see Putin and Trump as forceful counter-powers to the EU and the national elites rather than as ideological brethren. Their relationship is an impersonal marriage of convenience, driven more by common enemies than by common goals.

Whether Trump will establish indirect ties to Europe's far right leaders, as Putin has done through various low- and high-ranking politicians of his United Russia party, remains to be seen. There are definitely suitable candidates within the Republican Party: members of Congress like Louis Gohmert and Steve King have been meeting with European far right leaders like Le Pen and Wilders well before Trump took over the party. But they are hardly part of the inner circle of Trump.

The key questions for the coming years are going to be: How will Trump govern? Is he going to dominate the Republican Party, making it truly into *his* party, or is he going to work around the party and its (former) establishment? Based on his campaign, the latter is much more likely. Trump merely used the Republican Party to get access to the mediatized primary system and launch his campaign from within the mainstream rather than from the third-party margins. While the party establishment overall endorsed him, it remains a fragile and highly distrustful pact, which was mainly driven by a deep hatred for Hillary Clinton and an all-consuming appetite for power.

With Clinton defeated, and the Grand Old Party in control of all branches of government – including soon the Supreme Court – tensions will flare up again. Trump will probably continue to rely on a small group of outsiders, including former Republican darlings like ex-Speaker of the House Newt Gingrich and ex-Mayor of New York City Rudy Giuliani, who hold little sway in the current GOP. Rather than build a far right organization, inside or outside the Republican Party, by bringing in people from the so-called "alt-right," he will continue to normalize them by appearing in their media and parroting their propaganda.

There is one silver lining, however. While the Trump victory could further strengthen the already considerable momentum of the European far right in the coming months, it could come back to haunt them later on. Just as Brexit has decreased Euroskepticism in several European countries, the expected chaos of a Trump presidency could lead to a popular backlash to far right parties in Europe. This is even more so because both Brexit and Trump are not universally supported among far right supporters (or leaders, for that matter). This is the main reason why Europe's far right leaders are cautious in their embrace of Trump, celebrating the phenomenon rather than the man himself.

Note

1 This chapter was first published as "Europe's Far Right Has Been Boosted By Trump's Win – For Now" in the *Guardian* (9 November 2016).

24 Donald Trump is an American original

The major threat of a Trump presidency is Donald Trump's unpredictability, Dutch populism expert Cas Mudde tells Deutsche Welle. *The US-based professor also talks about a possible Trump effect on Austria's election.*[1]

DEUTSCHE WELLE: You have defined populism as an ideology that separates society into two homogeneous and antagonistic groups, "the pure people" and "the corrupt elite," and which says that politics should be an expression of "the general will" of the people. How does Trumpism, for lack of a better word, fit that mold?

CAS MUDDE: For most of his campaign it didn't really fit it, because – while he saw the elite as homogenous and corrupt and targeted both Republicans and Democrats – he didn't really say much about the people being pure. Most importantly he thought that politics should pretty much follow his will (see Chapter 10). Now in the last couple of months his campaign became much more populist and he actually presented himself more often as the voice of the silent majority and as the voice of the people.

DW: You argue that while comparisons between Donald Trump and European right-wing politicians are helpful, to be fully understood Trump must be seen as an American phenomenon. Why do you think that?

CM: One of the key things that made him attractive is this idea of him being a successful businessman. The US has a very strong tradition, particularly in the Republican Party, of believing that the president should be a kind of CEO of the United States who runs the country like a business. This is a very American view and not popular at all in Europe. I also think that the way he came up through the Republican Party and as a television personality are things that are much more pronounced and much more typical for the US than for Europe. In Europe almost all politicians that come through are representatives of a political party, often of a larger subculture. Trump is just an individual.

DW: But Donald Trump has achieved what many right-wing politicians in Europe have not yet – to lead a country. What do you expect of a Trump presidency and what role will the Republican Party play in this?

CM: It is very important to remember that Donald Trump was the radical right leader of a non-radical right party. You cannot really equate his support to someone like Marine Le Pen because a sizeable share of his voters, perhaps even a majority, just voted for the Republican Party and would maybe even have preferred to vote for a non-radical right leader of the Republican Party, but didn't have that option.

What I expect of a Trump presidency is a very, very right-wing GOP government. If you look at his appointments, especially those that have cabinet rank and therefore need confirmation, they are mostly people who come from the very conservative, pro-business, anti-abortion wing and seem to have been facilitated by a group called Heritage Action, which is a very conservative group linked to the Heritage Foundation. And that part will be completely successful because that part is completely in line with the GOP, which holds, of course, both houses of Congress.

On top of that you have Trump and some of his more esoteric advisors like Bannon, Flynn and others. They will push for less common agenda points, particularly with regard to foreign policy where they will push for a different US policy position on Russia and also for some type of isolationism, as well as perhaps some larger socio-economic projects like the infrastructure plan. I think they will find themselves largely unsuccessful, because they will find a Congress that is completely unresponsive.

The key point is: How does the world respond to, let's put it mildly, a very unorthodox president? And that is the major threat of the Trump presidency – his unpredictability.

DW: That was my next question, since you study populism and the extreme right. What can you tell us from your experience and research on how the world and the US should best deal with a President Trump?

CM: I don't think you really can learn any lessons because Trump is truly unique when compared to most other populist leaders in established democracies. He has no history and has no particular structure that ties him down. From that perspective he is really only kind of comparable to Silvio Berlusconi, who also was a one-man-party businessman with no real political ties. But the big difference is Trump is the president of the US and Berlusconi was the prime minister of Italy.

The problem with Trump is every tweet that he sends is world news because of his position. And given that he sends erratic messages, markets are going to respond, governments are going to respond and that is the big problem. The question will be: Will he learn and understand that whatever he does now has actual consequences in the real world? And I am skeptical about that if you look, for example, at his tweet storm from Sunday. It shows that he is still the same.

The lesson to learn is of course that everyone has to be vigilant, but also not to jump on everything. Because the other thing we learn is that he just spouts ideas and then moves on. Many things he said in the past are completely irrelevant today. So instead of panicking over every tweet it is crucial for the US and pretty much the rest of the world to take a step back and remember that this is Trump and wait to see what he does.

DW: In Austria's repeat presidential election next weekend a Green Party candidate will face a candidate of the right-wing Freedom Party. Do you expect a Trump effect?

CM: I don't expect a Trump effect, but I do expect Hofer [the Freedom Party candidate] to win. Europeans don't vote for far right candidates simply because Americans voted for Trump. They vote for radical right candidates for domestic reasons. And if you look at the polls, Hofer is up in most polls and he has been under-polled for the last year. So it seems logical to assume that he is going to win the presidency, but I don't think that Trump plays a major role in that.

The interview was conducted by Michael Knigge.

Note

1 This chapter was first published in *Deutsche Welle* (29 November 2016).

25 Trumpism
Normal pathology or pathological normalcy?

Many observers treat "Trumpism" as a pathology of US politics, unrelated to the ideologies of the political mainstream (i.e. the Democratic and Republican Parties) and at odds with the attitudes of the American people. But a closer look at elite discourse and mass attitudes paints a very difference picture.

Americans pride themselves on being democrats. For many, democracy is part of America, and some even believe it is unique to democracy. While other countries have democratic systems too, it was often only introduced reluctantly, after centuries of compromises or after a lost war and (American) occupation. This might explain the limited academic and political attention for the radical right in the US. While the topic is studied by hundreds of scholars from across the humanities and social sciences in Europe, few US colleagues have specialized on the topic (see also Chapter 18). But this wasn't always the case.

The anti-communist movement of the postwar period generated a significant scholarly output, including by prominent historians like Richard Hofstadter and social scientists like Daniel Bell and Seymour Martin Lipset. They published several essays and (edited) books on "the radical right," laying the groundwork for much of the European scholarship of the late 20th century (even if this is rarely acknowledged explicitly). Much of the scholarship was overtly political and did not just study but also denounced the radical right – another similarity with later European work. Influenced by the Frankfurt School's use of medical and psychological terminology, the radical right was pathologized. Most famously, Hofstadter described populism as "the paranoid style of politics."

25.1 The normal pathology thesis

The idea that radical right politics was a pathology of Western democracies was elaborated in more detail by two German social

Normal pathology or pathological normalcy? 89

scientists, Erwin Scheuch and Hans-Dieter Klingemann, who were both strongly influenced by the American scholarship on the radical right. In short, they argued that radical right politics was a normal pathology of Western democracies, meaning that radical right ideas were unrelated to democratic ideas, but a small part of the population in Western democracies still held these "residual," pre-democratic, ideas. Scheuch would later estimate the size of that group at 5 to 10 percent of the population. The thesis also held that this group could grow significantly (only) under conditions of a crisis, although the authors remained vague on what that meant – clearly, they were influenced here by their own national history, i.e. the rise of Adolf Hitler's Nazi party in the wake of the Great Depression.

Although almost no one has ever read Scheuch and Klingemann's seminal article, published only in German in a relatively obscure academic journal, the normal pathology thesis has dominated the academic and public understanding of the radical right since at least the 1960s. Radical right ideas are believed to be held just by a small part of the population, often dismissed as "hillbillies," or more recently "deplorables," and only become politically relevant during times of (economic or political) crisis – as is captured most popularly in the "losers of globalization" thesis (see Chapter 16).

Oddly enough, this thesis has never really been tested empirically. Its validity is assumed rather than proven. In an earlier study of the situation in Western Europe, however, it turned out that populist radical right ideas were not marginal within society. In fact, they were so widespread that the populist radical right is better seen as a pathological normalcy, i.e. a radicalization of mainstream ideas, than a normal pathology. Could this also be true in the United States, or is there really a case to be made for American exceptionalism? Let's assess that on the basis of the three core features of the populist radical right ideology (and Trumpism): nativism, authoritarianism, and populism.

25.2 Nativism

Simply stated, nativism is a xenophobic form of nationalism, incorporating the idea that countries should be inhabited exclusively by members of the native group ("the nation") and that nonnative elements (persons and ideas) are fundamentally threatening to the homogeneous nation-states. It is best summarized in the infamous German slogan "*Deutschland den Deutschen! Ausländer raus!*" ("Germany for the Germans. Foreigners Out!"). At first sight, nativism seems to run counter to the American spirit, as the US defines itself as "a nation of immigrants." But there have been many heated debates about which "immigrants" are, and which are not, welcome in the US.

For a long time, most political elites agreed that the US was a nation of (only) white Anglo-Saxon Protestant (WASP) immigrants. This led not just to an overall racist immigration policy, with notorious policies like the Chinese Exclusion Act (1882), but also nativist policies and riots targeting white Europeans who were Catholic (see Chapter 2). Today, nativist organizations like the Federation for American Immigration Reform (FAIR) prioritize all white Christian Europeans, which they, with little sense of irony, define as the "native Americans." While this more or less white nationalist position is not mainstream, at least not explicitly, nativism is an important part of the US political discourse, as could most recently be seen in the implementation of anti-immigration legislation in a range of states.

The overall more pro-immigrant and -immigration elite discourse is shared by large parts of the US population – compared to Western, and particularly Eastern, Europe. For example, a recent AP-NORC poll on "The American Identity" found that 65 percent of Americans say diversity makes the US stronger, while 61 percent say legal immigration boosts the US reputation as a land of opportunity and benefits companies with technical expertise. At the same time, there are significant minorities, and sometimes even pluralities or majorities, that hold more or less explicitly nativist attitudes. One-third of Americans think "a culture established by the country's early European immigrants" is extremely/very important to American identity (40 percent say moderately important), and 40 percent think the same of "a culture grounded in Christian religious beliefs" (25 percent moderately important). Moreover, 47 percent of Americans think illegal immigration is extremely/very threatening to the American way of life (25 percent moderately threatening), while 15 percent think legal immigration is (23 percent moderately threatening).

25.3 Authoritarianism

Authoritarianism is the belief in a strictly ordered society in which infringements of authority are to be punished severely. Most notably, "love and respect for authority," a euphemistic description of authoritarianism, is considered to be a core staple of conservatism and various strands of Christianity. Not surprising, then, that authoritarianism is a core ideological feature of the Republican Party, which has sought law and order solutions for most social issues – think about the "War on Drugs" – and has been the prime party responsible for the, by the standards of other Western democracies, draconian policies – including three-strikes-out, minimum sentences and, of course, the death penalty. However, it is important to note that many of these authoritarian measures are also supported by Democratic elites, particularly in the "American Heartland" of the Midwest and South.

Authoritarian attitudes are also widespread among the US population: roughly half of the US population can be classified as "authoritarian" based on various surveys.[1] Not surprisingly, given the omnipresent celebration of law enforcement and military forces, the army and the police are among the most trusted institutions in the US. And while numbers have been falling for years now, in 2014 a majority of Americans believed local courts were too lenient on criminals and supported the death penalty for murderers. In addition, within the framework of counter-terrorism policies, Americans have become quite accepting of authoritarian policies. In 2006, 47 percent supported the use of wiretaps without a warrant and 65 percent believed the media should not report on secret methods in the fight against terrorism. A disturbing 23 percent even thought it was not okay to criticize the president on the fight against terrorism.

25.4 Populism

The third and final feature, populism, is a thin-centered ideology that considers society to be ultimately separated into two homogeneous and antagonistic groups, "the pure people" versus "the corrupt elite," and argues that politics should be an expression of the *volonté générale*, i.e. the general will of the people. Unlike Western Europe, North America has a long populist tradition, going back to the popular interpretation of the Founding Fathers, who allegedly believed in the power of "We the People." While populist movements have rarely been able to become a national political force, they date back to the mid-19th century, and have been major players at the regional level in various periods. Moreover, mild forms of populism are part of every political campaign – think about the distinction between "Main Street" (pure) and "Wall Street" (corrupt) – and much of the political culture – from Thomas Paine's pamphlet *Common Sense* (1776), through Frank Capra's classic movie *Mr. Smith Goes to Washington* (1939), to John Rich's anti-bailout country song *Shuttin' Detroit Down* (2009).

It will come as no surprise that anti-establishment sentiments are widespread among Americans. Trust in key political institutions is at all-time lows, with trust in Congress in the single digits. Almost three-quarters of Americans believe that most elected officials put their own interests ahead of the country's interests, while just 19 percent say they trust the federal government always or most of the time. Just 29 percent of Americans think elected officials are honest, while 48 percent think they lazy and 72 percent think they are selfish. In short, Americans hold strong anti-establishment sentiments. But are they populist?

Until recently we had few indicators to measure populism (as defined here) at the mass level. But recent studies show that most Americans can be labeled mildly or strongly populist. For example, some 80 percent of Americans think that the politicians in Congress need to follow the will of the people, more than 70 percent believe that the power of a few special interests prevents the country from making progress, and almost half of Americans hold that politics is ultimately a struggle between good and evil.[2] To be clear, all these positions could also be held by non-populists, and many Americans combine them with support for pluralist attitudes (which are, theoretically, opposed to populism), but they show at the very least that many Americans are open to populist ideas.

Interestingly, while attitudes toward the party system have grown consistently more negative, this does not hold for attitudes toward political parties. The most plausible explanation is the recent rise of polarization within US society, particularly, but not exclusively, among Republicans. Interestingly, this polarization might also weaken, or at the very least transform, populist attitudes. Pew Research Center recently found that almost two-thirds of Americans believe "their side" loses more often than it wins in politics, and that all Americans, including non-partisans, have lost confidence and trust in the public's political wisdom – in 2007 57 percent had at least a good deal of confidence in the political wisdom of the people, while in 2015 63 percent had little or no confidence.[3]

25.5 Trumpism: a pathological normalcy

This short, and necessarily coarse, overview shows that "Trumpism" is not a normal pathology of contemporary US society. The core features of the populist radical right ideology have long been expressed by elites and are still supported by significant parts of the masses, albeit sometimes in less radical versions. Compared to Western Europe, nativism is less widespread and, perhaps even more importantly, countered by a more dominant pro-immigration and pro-immigrant narrative – although who the "good" immigrants are is debated to this day. On authoritarianism and particularly populism, however, US society beats Western European societies.

Now one can argue that the fact that core features of the populist radical right ideology are supported by large minorities, if not pluralities or even outright majorities, of US society does not necessarily disqualify the normal pathology thesis. Aren't we living in a time of economic crisis? There are two arguments against this defense. First, it is hard to argue that US society is still in an economic crisis. While the Great Recession hit the US hard, this was in 2008, and the bailouts at the very least changed the mood and narrative about, if not perhaps the underlying economic reasons for, the crisis. Unlike Southern Europe, for example, the US has not officially been in an economic crisis since at least 2010.

This doesn't mean that significant parts of the population are not still experiencing the impact of the Great Recession, or that they *think* the US is in an economic crisis. In fact, surveys showed that during the 2016 presidential election campaign many Americans felt that the US economy was in a bad state – even if they didn't necessarily think their personal economic situation was bad. This was primarily the case among people who (strongly) identified as Republicans. The number fell significantly just days after Trump was elected president, which shows the partisan bias of the assessment, but does not necessarily mean it didn't genuinely influence their political behavior.

A more convincing refutation of the crisis argument is that many of these attitudes were even more widespread before the Great Recession. Both nativism and authoritarianism have overall been declining in the US, sometimes for decades. And while populism might be even higher now than it was before the economic crisis, it is a constituent part of US political culture and has been around during times of crisis *and* boom. In other words, and with some qualification (with regard to nativism), Trumpism is a pathological normalcy in the US, a radicalization of mainstream views. This means not only that Trump did not come "out of nowhere," but also that Trumpism won't disappear with Trump. That said, two of its core features, nativism and authoritarianism, are becoming less popular, at least at the mass level, meaning that as a majoritarian strategy at the federal level, Trumpism is on its last legs.

Notes

1 See, for instance, the fundamental study of authoritarianism in the US, Marc J. Hetherington and Jonathan D. Weiler, *Authoritarianism and Polarization in American Politics* (New York: Cambridge University Press, 2009).
2 See Kirk Hawkins, Scott Riding and Cas Mudde, "Measuring Populist Attitudes," *Committee on Concepts and Methods Working Paper Series*, No. 55, 2012.
3 See "Beyond Distrust: How Americans View Their Government," available at www.people-press.org/2015/11/23/beyond-distrust-how-americans-view-their-government (last consulted on 11 May 2017).

26 Donald Trump and the silent counter-revolution

In 1992 the Italian political scientist Piero Ignazi wrote an influential article, arguing that the rise of Europe's "extreme right" parties was the consequence of a "silent counter-revolution." While the thesis has some merit in Europe, it might be better applied to the recent rise of Trump(ism) in the US.

Most US commentators consider Donald Trump as the American representative of a broader Western phenomenon, i.e. the rise of "populist" or "far right" politics, but few of them are aware of the over three decades of academic research that explains this rise. Rather than drawing upon the hundreds of scholarly books and thousands of academic articles on the radical right in Europe,[1] they reinvent the wheel over and over again, presenting decades-old theories as path-breaking and generalizing on the basis of an N=1, while we *know* that similar statements have been proven wrong in many other countries.

26.1 Explanations for the 2016 presidential election

First, as the US political scientist Larry Bartels has convincingly argued, "2016 was an ordinary election, not a realignment" (*Washington Post*, 10 November 2016). Roughly 90 percent of people with a party identification voted for that party. In other words, Democrats voted Democrat, Republicans Republican!

Second, as far as there was indeed a significant group of "new" Trump voters, i.e. former non-voters or Democrats who switched to Trump, they will hardly constitute an enigma for the informed analyst. The low-educated, white, working-class male was already identified as the stereotypical radical right voter in Europe in the mid-1990s. Their main motivations are a toxic mix of authoritarianism, economic anxiety, and political dissatisfaction, all strongly shaped by an overarching nativism (see also Chapter 16).

The more interesting question is not so much how Trump could beat Clinton, but how Trump could become the leader of the mainstream right-wing party. Leaving aside the specific context of the primaries – i.e. an exceptionally large field of unknown and unpopular candidates – Trump was in many ways also the candidate most representative of the attitudes and issues of most Republican (primary) voters. Trump didn't hijack the GOP (see Chapter 19), the GOP handed the party to him!

26.2 The silent counter-revolution thesis

To explain how that happened, we should turn to, in my opinion, the best article ever written on the radical right. In 1992, the Italian political scientist Piero Ignazi wrote an article entitled "The Silent Counter-Revolution: Hypotheses on the Emergence of Extreme Right-Wing Parties in Europe,"[2] which introduced an original theory to explain what was at that time the still modest electoral success of far right parties in Western Europe. While it has limitations within a European context, I believe it provides unique insights into the US context.

Ignazi notes that, at that time, existing theories didn't account for the rise of "extreme right-wing" parties. In fact, their success ran contra one of the most important theories of the time, the "silent revolution" of US political scientist Ronald Inglehart, who, simply stated, argued that a variety of economic and societal changes – most notably peace and affluence – had created a generation in the West that were no longer concerned by materialist issues (like the economy and security) and instead focused on so-called post-materialist values, such as identity and solidarity.[3] Inglehart used this theory to explain the rise of the new social movements of the 1970s, including the gay and women's as well as the international solidarity movements, but also the Green parties of the 1980s.

But where Inglehart predicted growing popularity of these progressive movements, Green parties were increasingly overshadowed by far right parties, in many ways their ideological opposites. To explain this, Ignazi takes Inglehart a step further, arguing that the far right is a direct reaction to the success of the Greens and progressive post-materialist politics; hence, a silent counter-revolution. However, the reaction is not direct. It is mitigated through the rise of neoconservatism in the 1980s.

Ignazi argues that the original right-wing reaction to the silent revolution was the rise of neoconservatism in the 1980s, with politicians like Margaret Thatcher in the UK and Ronald Reagan in the US, which re-emphasized authority, patriotism, the role of the family and traditional moral values. This "provoked, directly or indirectly, a higher polarization both in terms of ideological distance and in terms of ideological intensity." Moreover, this radicalization led to a decline in party identification and, *in extremis*, in identification with the political system. It is in this new political context that the far right becomes a viable option, particularly when the mainstream right moves back to the center out of fear of losing centrist voters.

26.3 Neoconservatives and polarization in the US

This process barely played out in Europe, because, with perhaps the exception of the UK, neoconservatism never really took hold of the mainstream right-wing parties. But it certainly did in the US, where conservatism was transformed during Reagan's presidency, through an exceptionally strong neoconservative infrastructure of magazines (e.g. *Commentary, Weekly Standard*) and think tanks (e.g. American Enterprise Institute, Heritage Foundation). When Ronald Reagan declared, famously, in his 1981 inaugural speech, "government is not the solution to the problem, it is the problem," it was considered a controversial and radical statement. Today, it is received wisdom within the Republican Party (and among many of my students).

Scholars and pundits have noted how politics in the US Congress has polarized radically over the past decades. The polarization is partly measured in terms of party loyalty, i.e. how often individual members of Congress toe the party line, as well as ideological extremity.[4] But while party loyalty can be observed on both sides of the political aisle, ideological radicalization is primarily a Republican affair. As think tankers Thomas E. Mann and Norman J. Ornstein wrote in the first edition of their best-selling book, *It's Even Worse Than It Looks* (2012):

> The Republican Party has become an insurgent outlier – ideologically extreme; contemptuous of the inherited social and economic policy regime; scornful of compromise; unpersuaded by conventional understanding of facts, evidence, and science; and dismissive of the legitimacy of its political opposition.

While the neoconservative turn challenged the status quo from the beginning, it soon created a new equilibrium, helped by the right-wing turn of the Democratic Party under President Bill Clinton.

The Republican party leadership would continue to use a radical discourse on both socio-economic (e.g. deregulation and taxation) and socio-cultural issues (e.g. abortion and affirmative action), but they never fundamentally challenged the political order and system. However, parts of its support base and donors did take the radical discourse seriously and demanded (more) radical policies. They came together in the Tea Party, which attacked the RINOs (Republicans In Name Only), and replaced some of them with inexperienced newcomers, pushing the boundaries of the party and the system. The revolution was starting to eat its children, as was probably best exemplified by the government shutdown in 2013 (see Chapter 7). In many ways, the new Tea Party members of Congress simply followed through on the Republican Party's longstanding rhetorical demands, putting the party establishment in an awkward position, squeezed between angry voters and upset donors.

Predictably, the party leadership chose "responsibility" over "responsiveness," in the terms of the late Irish political scientist Peter Mair,[5] enraging its now mobilized radical base. With the GOP leadership discredited, and the new Tea Party Caucus shown too weak, they were looking for a new champion of their populist revolt, which they found in an unlikely, but eventually very effective, person: Donald Trump. Trump was not a traditional conservative, not even a real Republican, but he personified the radical and uncompromising politics of the Tea Party more than its former representatives, like Marco Rubio and Ted Cruz. He was willing to fundamentally change the system, and even break it if necessary. Moreover, the system, from liberals to establishment conservatives (like blogger Erick Erickson and the *National Review*), denounced him vehemently, thereby showing his supporters that he was the real deal.

26.4 Trump and Reagan

While it is too strong to argue that Donald Trump is the true successor to Ronald Reagan, he definitely is to a large extent the outcome of an ideological transformation of the Republican Party that gained real traction during Reagan's presidency – to be fair, in terms of racialized politics, it even goes back to President Richard Nixon and the so-called Southern strategy.[6] Decades of increasingly radical rhetoric, and to a slightly lesser extent policies, created expectations that were at direct odds with the interests of the GOP establishment. When the latter finally caved to the pressures of "responsible" politics, and the internal upstarts proved powerless to stop it, space opened up for an outsider who had no loyalty to the party establishment or political status quo. Because of the pressures of the two-party system, as well as the "open tent strategy" of the Republican Party, the outsider decided to challenge the system from within one of its main political pillars, ironically making it more representative of its (primary) base.

Notes

1 A good start would be my recent edited volume *The Populist Radical Right: A Reader* (London: Routledge, 2017), which brings together 32 seminal articles and book chapters from the past three decades. See also Chapter 33 in this book.
2 The article appeared in a special issue on "extreme right-wing parties in Europe" of the *European Journal of Political Research* and is included in the above-mentioned reader.
3 See Ronald Inglehart, *The Silent Revolution: Changing Values and Political Styles Among Western Publics* (Princeton, NJ: Princeton University Press, 1977).
4 The most recent version of the foundational study of the process of polarization is Nolan McCarty, Keith T. Poole and Howard Rosenthal, *Polarized America: The Dance of Ideology and Unequal Riches* (Cambridge, MA: MIT Press, 2016).
5 See Peter Mair, *Ruling the Void: The Hollowing of Western Democracy* (London: Verso, 2013).
6 On the importance of the Southern strategy in the transformation of the Republican Party, see Joseph E. Lowndes, *From the New Deal to the New Right* (New Haven, CT: Yale University Press, 2008).

27 What's the matter with America?
Trump and the multidimensionality of politics

In 2016 all four parties that dominate the two-party systems in the UK and US faced intense internal divisions. Rather than the results of the appearance of some colorful personalities, like Donald Trump, they are the consequence of the evolution of the political system into a highly complex three-dimensional space, which provides a fundamental challenge to "big tent" parties like the GOP.

The 2016 primary and presidential election have opened the US up to the world. I have never seen so many references to politics in other countries than at this time. While American exceptionalism hasn't totally been discarded, journalists and pundits are eagerly looking across the borders to make sense of some unexpected developments. Not surprisingly, the focus is on Europe, in particular on the larger European countries, the only ones that at least get some coverage in US media.

27.1 Sanders, Trump, and their (alleged) European counterparts

Most commentators have noted the similarities of Donald Trump and former Italian Prime Minister Silvio Berlusconi, both right-wing populists, both very rich, old men with a history of sexism and access to unprecedented free media. But Trump has also been compared to (Jean-Marie and Marine) Le Pen, leaders of the French National Front (FN). Here the alleged similarity is primarily in terms of ideology, i.e. they share a core ideology (or at least platform) of nativism, authoritarianism, and populism (see Chapter 9). But there are similarities on the left as well, between Bernie Sanders and Jeremy Corbyn, the new leader of the British Labour Party.

Sanders and Corbyn are both "insider-outsiders" who challenged the party establishment from within. How that challenges some of the key theories in US political science will be discussed in the next chapter.

100 What's the matter with America?

Unlike Trump, both Corbyn and Sanders have long functioned more or less within the parties they are now (trying to) take over, although Sanders was an "independent" part of the Democratic faction in the Senate. They (re)presented a "radical left" alternative against the center-left (which really is center or center-right) party establishment. In the autumn of their lives they became the hope of a new generation of left-wing youths, who had only a tangential connection to their parties.

All three are also symptoms of the deep divisions within the mainstream parties of the UK and US. Like Corbyn and Sanders, Trump has shown that the GOP is really two parties – a traditional conservative party, strongest at the elite level, and a radical right party, strongest at the mass level (see Chapter 19). In fact, one could argue that Ron and Rand Paul have showed that the GOP is really three parties, but the libertarian part has little support at either the elite or the mass level.

27.2 The multidimensionality of contemporary politics

This speaks to the multidimensionality of contemporary politics. Although we always speak in terms of "left" and "right" politics, or in the US context about "conservative" and "liberal" politics, these terms have long referred to at least two different dimensions: the socio-economic and the socio-cultural dimensions. The socio-economic dimension centers on the role of the state in the economy, pitting a free market right against a state intervention left. It has come to dominate Western politics after the Industrial Revolution and constitutes the core of the old party systems. But it has lost relevance, as a consequence of an increasing embrace of the market by center-left parties and the rise of non- or post-material issues (see Chapter 26).

The socio-cultural dimension might be better seen as constituting two dimensions itself, i.e. the authoritarian-libertarian and the cosmopolite-nationalist. The former refers to state intervention in the personal life, referring not just to whether the state should ban certain behavior but also whether it should instill and protect certain (traditional) values. In the US this dimension is particularly related to political issues like abortion, the death penalty, and drugs, and it is strongly correlated with religiosity. Authoritarians want the state to actively intervene in these issues, while libertarians want the state to butt out and let citizens make their own choices. This time the pro-state side is seen as conservative/right, and the anti-state side as liberal/left.

In recent decades a second socio-cultural dimension has gained relevance, which pits cosmopolites against nationalists. Cosmopolites favor international cooperation and integration, believe in values that transcend national boundaries (like "liberal" or "global" values), and favor relatively open borders for people, goods, and values. Nationalists want to protect their own national interests and values by more or less closed borders and minimal international cooperation and involvement. The national interest tops all other concerns. Nationalists are considered to be conservative/right, cosmopolites liberal/left.

27.3 The GOP in a multidimensional world

In this three-dimensional world, all political parties are internally divided. Logically, parties in two-party systems like the UK and US are particularly affected. The GOP is trying to be a "big tent" for all right-wing forces, but what is "right wing" depends on the dimension. The current party establishment, influenced by neoconservatism, is right on the socio-economic (market) and first socio-cultural dimension (authoritarian), but more left on the second socio-cultural dimension (cosmopolitan). The Pauls are right on the socio-economic dimension (market), more left on the first socio-cultural dimension (libertarian, though not on abortion), and right on the second socio-cultural dimension.

Trump has offered a combination to the GOP that has been completely marginalized by the dominance of neoconservatism within the party. In many ways, it is similar to the paleoconservative platform of Patrick "Pat" Buchanan, who unsuccessfully sought the presidential nomination in 1992 and 1996, before standing as a third-party candidate for the Reform Party in 2000. It is doubtful that Trump is aware of Buchanan, and there are no clear ties between the two camps – although both have a connection to the MSNBC TV show *Morning Joe* of former Republican House member Joe Scarborough.

Trump combines a somewhat inconsistent position on the socio-economic dimension, supporting both a massive state-sponsored infrastructure project and radical deregulation of business, with a very rightwing position on both socio-cultural dimensions, based on his strong authoritarianism and nativism. This is the same combination that has made populist radical right parties like the Austrian Freedom Party (FPÖ) and FN attractive in Europe, particularly to white working class voters outside the urban centers. It is also not that dissimilar to the agenda of the Dixiecrats, which has been mostly integrated into the Republican Party in the South, but not at the federal level. Not surprisingly, Trump has appointed quite a lot of Southern Republicans to his cabinet.

Trump's radical right position connects the GOP much better to its core electorate than the neoconservatism of the GOP establishment. As Thomas Frank has argued in his influential book *What's the Matter with*

Kansas? (2005), the GOP must downplay the socio-economic dimension in campaigns to win over the white middle class on the basis of socio-cultural issues – most notably on the first dimension, i.e. abortion. While Frank's thesis is not without critics, who claim it is overstated and that class does still play an important role in party politics, there is no doubt that Trump's more flexible position on the socio-economic dimension, as well as his emphasis on the second socio-cultural dimension (i.e. immigration instead of abortion), is a much better fit for the white middle class. But it probably has a shorter shelf life.

27.4 The post-Trump strategy

In essence, Trump's agenda is a white strategy on steroids, mobilizing the white working class at the expense of pretty much all non-white voters. By prioritizing nativism over all other issues, even conservative and nationalist non-white Americans have a hard time embracing a Trump GOP. In a country where more and more states will become majority-minority in the coming decade, including in the Southeast (e.g. Florida and Georgia), this is a short-term strategy, where the long-term costs to the party will outweigh the short-term benefits many times over.

The neoconservative strategy of the past decades has problems as well, particularly for the attraction of better-educated, younger, white conservatives. These groups are much more libertarian on issues like gay and women's rights as well as legalization of marijuana. This is not the case on the issue of abortion, however, where younger Republicans are still more authoritarian, but don't prioritize it. At the same time, the radical neoconservative interventionist foreign policy agenda is less important to and supported by younger as well as non-white Republicans. But a more moderate conservative agenda – which includes support for small and medium-sized businesses, "family values," and regulated immigration – would not only appeal to better-educated, young, white Republicans but could also allow the GOP to finally make significant inroads into the non-white population, particularly Asian Americans and Hispanics.

In short, while Trump has been able to match the GOP to its core constituency in a new, complex three-dimensional political space, this has been at the expense of almost all other electorates. Given the changing demographics of the US, this strategy can only have short-term success – barring massive new measures of disenfranchisement of mostly non-white voters. Long-term, the GOP will have to go beyond the angry white vote, which will mean reaching out to non-white voters by moderating its position on all three dimensions of US politics.

28 Did Trump prove US political science wrong?

After the surprise election of Donald Trump many journalists and pundits gloated over the alleged failure of political scientists to predict the outcome. This was the crown on months of critical discussions of two of the most popular theories in the study of US elections, i.e. those focusing on the role of money and of the party. But did these theories really fail? And what does that mean for the future study of US elections?

To call Donald Trump's election a surprise is an understatement. Virtually all prediction models gave Hillary Clinton solid odds to win the presidency, some close to 100 percent, as did almost all pundits. While the national polls were overall more accurate, many correctly predicting a Clinton win in the popular vote of a few percentage points, most were wrong in the key states that in the end decided Trump's victory in the Electoral College. Some of the prediction models based on the so-called "fundamentals," a static combination of economic and political indicators like incumbency and the state of the economy, did predict a Trump win, but didn't necessarily get right the difference between the popular vote loss and Electoral College win.

Most prediction models and polls are atheoretical, i.e. they are not based on a theoretical model, and their reputation and weighing are mainly based on previous predictions. If there is anything we can learn from the victory of Trump, it is that the extremely low response rate is creating major problems for polls – not just in the US – and that pollsters need to rethink their margins of error, which were established when polls had much higher response rates. Today, many polls have a response rate of just 10 percent, which means that only one in ten of the people who are contacted actually participate in the poll, and the usual margin of error is +/- 3 percent, which means that there is a 6 percent margin around a number. In other words, if Trump is polled at 48 percent, it really means that the pollster is certain that his support is between 45 and 51 percent.

104 Did Trump prove US political science wrong?

But political science is, or at least should be, about explanations, not predictions. How did US political science do theoretically in terms of the 2016 presidential election? There were two political science theories that received particular coverage in the run-up to the election, and which were taken to task after Trump's surprise win. The first holds that the party decides, which relates mainly to the stage of primaries, while the second argues that money decides, which applies to both stages of the presidential election.

28.1 The Party Decides

Few political science books are so well-cited (though probably much less well-read) by US journalists than *The Party Decides* (2008),[1] which, simply stated, argues that, despite caucuses and primaries in which party loyalists can vote for the official party candidate, the two big US parties continue to strictly control the process through so-called "invisible primaries." The argument is that party elites, as well as powerful brokers in the supportive subculture around the party, still control the outcome "by sending cues and signals," of which official endorsements are among the most powerful.

According to many journalists, as well as some political scientists, the victory of Trump in the GOP primaries proves that, at the very least, the party *no longer* decides. After all, almost all major voices within the party leadership initially supported another candidate in the primaries – one notable exception was Alabama Senator Jeff Sessions – and many openly came out against Trump. And while the #NeverTrump movement never really took off, most of the leading voices in the GOP and its support structure kept support from Trump until his defeat was mathematically impossible. Moreover, Donald Trump received no major endorsements until well after the first primaries and finished with just 46 official endorsements from GOP Congress members and governors. This was not only a fraction of what previous GOP presidential nominees had received – Mitt Romney had more than ten times as many (475) in 2012 and John McCain almost seven times as many (303) in 2008 – but also (far) fewer than his three main challengers in 2016 – Florida Senator Marco Rubio (139), Texas Senator Ted Cruz (114), and Ohio Governor John Kasich (48).

Unsurprisingly, after taking *The Party Decides* as gospel for much of the primary, the media were quick to savage it as soon as Trump had secured the GOP nomination. While some journalists acknowledged that most media present a caricature of the main argument of *The Party Decides*, even they argued that the authors were wrong, at least on the 2016 GOP primary. Even one of the authors, Marty Cohen, admitted being surprised by the outcome, suggesting celebrities and social media had transformed the primary process, undermining the power of party elites. Political scientist and *Washington Post* blogger Dan Drezner went so far as to suggest that *The Party Decides* had made political elites complacent about the run of Trump to the extent that they only realized the book was wrong when it was too late.

28.2 Money talks

The second popular political science theory has a much longer history than *The Party Decides*. For decades political scientists have stressed the importance of money in US elections, at every level. The controversial Supreme Court's "Citizens United" decision of 2010, which (simply stated) removed important restrictions on private campaign donations, was met with apocalyptic despair by many Americans, who were afraid that it would unleash an explosion of (corporate) money in US elections. Many liberals proclaimed that Citizens United would mean the end of democracy and that the infamous Koch Brothers, two wealthy industrials who are among the main conservative donors in the US, would simply buy election outcomes.

Interestingly, the amount of money spent in the presidential elections spiked most in 2008, because of the unprecedented money of the Obama campaign. In the first presidential election after Citizens United, in 2012, Barack Obama spent slightly less, but his Republican challenger, Mitt Romney, spent more than twice as much as John McCain did in 2008. Contrary to all expectations, both Clinton and Trump spent much less in 2016 than Obama and Romney had done in 2012. Their campaigns and political action committees (PACs) together spent about half of the total amount of 2012. Clinton's war chest was more similar to that of John Kerry in 2004 (in terms of normalized dollars) than that of Obama in 2008 or 2012, who spend almost 50 percent more in both elections. Most shockingly, Trump was among the lowest spending Republicans candidates in the postwar era, even being outspent by Richard Nixon and Barry Goldwater in the 1960s (again, in terms of normalized dollars).

There is no doubt that Clinton outspent Trump in the 2016 elections; in fact, she did so pretty much throughout the whole campaign. In total Clinton raised a staggering $1.4 billion, while Trump mustered "only" $932 million. Her personal campaign raised almost twice as much as Trump's ($623 million versus $329 million), while her Super PACs raised more than twice as much as his ($204 million versus $79 million). Trump could only somewhat match Clinton in funds from party and joint fundraising committees ($524 million and $594 million, respectively).

Moreover, during most of the primary Trump was also outspent by his main Republican opponents. The last standing serious opponent, Ted Cruz, spent $86 million against Trump's $63 million, a good one-third more. Even more shocking, Ben Carson had spent almost twice as much as Trump when he dropped his bid in early March ($61 million versus $33 million). Even "Little" Marco Rubio had spent $4 million more by the time he bowed out in March.

28.3 In search of new theories?

There is little doubt that these two popular theories in US political science are unable to account for Trump's success in both the GOP primaries and the US presidential election of 2016. Trump received far fewer endorsements and spent much less money than his competitors, yet defeated both the other Republicans and Hillary Clinton. The question to be answered then, is whether Trump is the exception to the old rule, or is the new rule. There are good reasons to argue the former.

As has been well-established, candidates spend most of their campaign money on buying air time, most notably on cable TV. Trump received disproportional media coverage throughout both the primaries and presidential campaigns. Already in March 2016 the *New York Times* calculated that Trump had received the equivalent of $2 billion in free media. The total is believed to have been in the $5 billion area by election day. This was a consequence of several separate, but mutually strengthening, factors: 1) Trump had a uniquely high name recognition, particularly because of his popular TV show *The Apprentice*; 2) he was always available for major news networks; and 3) he was faced with a exceptionally large field of little-known and fairly unpopular competitors.

It is highly unlikely that a similar combination will present itself again. It would be the equivalent of Kanye West or Kim Kardashian contesting a post-Clinton Democratic Party primary. Moreover, while *The Party Decides* failed to explain the Clinton defeat against Trump, it perfectly explains her victory over Bernie Sanders. Clinton and Sanders were quite close in terms of votes, but they were worlds apart in terms of official endorsements as well as superdelegate votes.

In short, it is far too early to dismiss these theories, and throw out the baby with the bathwater. Instead, we should treat them like all social science theories should be treated, i.e. as probabilistic statements rather than natural laws, and try to improve them, by clarifying the conditions under which they do and do not hold.

Note

1 Marty Cohen, David Karol, Hans Noel and John Zaller, *The Party Decides: Presidential Nominations Before and After Reform* (Chicago, IL: The University of Chicago Press, 2008).

29 The politics of nostalgia

From the radical left to the radical right, the political status quo in Western democracies is challenged by a politics of nostalgia, which harks back to an (imagined) past. While nostalgia might provide comfort for the present, it does not inspire for the future.[1]

The political decisions of 2016 will influence our future for many years, if not decades, to come and yet they were primarily influenced by the past. From Nigel Farage's "We want our country *back*" in the British EU referendum to Donald Trump's "Make America Great *Again*" in the US presidential election, the emphasis was on a glorious past, sold as the blueprint of a magnificent future. This is the politics of nostalgia, which informs the main challengers of Western democracies today, from the radical right to the radical left.

What Mr. Farage and Mr. Trump are selling is not the 1930s, as alarmists frequently proclaim, but the 1950s. The period of the "Greatest Generation," who overcame the Great Depression and the Second World War to build the great country these populist leaders, and many of their followers, grew up in. An America or Britain in which there was a clear order, non-whites and women "knew their place," and white working class males made a decent living doing an honest day's work.

While this was a racist world, particularly in the Jim Crow South, the right-wing populist nostalgia is for a racialized rather than racist past. For the white supporters of these populist tribunes, most of whom were not around at the time, the 1950s was a glorious period of harmony between the races and sexes before affirmative action and political correctness stirred up emotions and disrupted the natural situation. Hence, accusations of racism meet with angry responses, as most right-wing populist supporters genuinely abhor outright racism and do not realize that their white privilege depends upon it.

Surveys find broad support for this type of nostalgia, particularly when it is not phrased in ostensibly racist terms. For example, among white evangelicals, one of the strongest supporter groups of Mr. Trump, a staggering 74 percent said that American life and culture "has mostly changed for the worse" since the 1950s. As Anthea Butler summarized these findings in *Religion Dispatches* (25 October 2015): "The upshot of this survey is that white evangelicals want to go back to Ozzie and Harriet – in time, behavior, and gender roles."

But the politics of nostalgia is not limited to the radical right. Two of the main beacons of the so-called "radical left," Jeremy Corbyn and Bernie Sanders, also find inspiration for their future ambitions in a slightly less distant past. Referring to a somewhat similar period, though also including the 1970s, they mostly emphasize different points. While both Mr. Sanders and Mr. Trump herald the well-paying (white) working class jobs of the past, only the former also lauds the strengths of the trade unions and the public sector. They both defend institutions of the welfare state that the Greatest Generation profited from, such as the National Health Service (NHS) in the UK and Social Security in the US.

The main message is: it used to be better (rather than it gets better). Take this telling statement by Mr. Sanders, at a rally in Bloomington, Indiana, in April 2016:

> Forty years ago, in this country, before the explosion of technology and cell phones, and space-age technology and all that stuff, before the explosion of the global economy, one person in a family – one person – could work forty hours a week and earn enough money to take care of the whole family.

Of course, both the left and the right refer to a past that, in their description, does not and has never existed. The politics of nostalgia exaggerates positive aspects and eliminates negative ones. The past is whitewashed. Just as Mr. Trump does not mention the lynchings of the 1950s, Mr. Sanders doesn't emphasize the patriarchal structure that sustained the families of that period. It is an imagined past, where people knew and trusted each other, still believed in their country, and weren't divided over identities and partisanship. Never mind the fact that people were literally fighting in the streets over the closing of the mines or the Vietnam War.

The politics of nostalgia is of all ages but it is particularly popular today. In the past decades politicians were mostly forward-looking, creating a new world order through innovative new international institutions like the European Union, International Monetary Fund, and United Nations. Many of these institutions were the direct result of a deeply held belief that the past should not repeat itself. The founding fathers of the EU were inspired by the postwar motto "Never Again," and the first supranational institution, the European Coal and Steel Community, was an explicit attempt to keep Germany and France from going to war again. Similarly, the United Nations was founded to prevent another world war and shaped by the failed experience of the largely ineffective League of Nations.

The reasons for the contemporary success of the politics of nostalgia are manifold. Yes, the Great Recession has profoundly affected optimism about the future, including among the youth, but in many ways was more a catalyst than the main cause. Nostalgic politics, particularly in its right-wing populist form, was already on the rise well before the economic crisis. More than anything, it is the consequence of the growing intellectual vacuum that dominates party politics in today's world. After the last great leap forward, inspired by neoliberalism, and accepted from the center-right to the center-left, we have slowly but steadily moved into a world of pragmatism and technocracy, in which expertise has replaced ideas.

When established politicians no longer offer attractive visions of the future, people look for solace in the past. They will let themselves be seduced by an imaginary public past that is mostly in line with their own imagined private past anyway. It is easy to dismiss this nostalgia as naïve and racist, which definitely play a role, but that will not bring back these voters – or prevent others from joining them. Many know that the reality was different, and some will even acknowledge the ugly racism of that period, but they will not abandon the politics of nostalgia until credible and dedicated politicians will again offer an attractive and convincing forward-looking program. As long as that is still in the future, they will continue to live in the past, while their leaders determine our present.

Note

1 This chapter was first published in *Newsweek* (15 December 2016).

30 2016 and the five stages of liberal denial

The unexpected victories of Brexit and Donald Trump have led to an outpouring of liberal despair in the (social) media, which in its most extreme form illustrates profoundly illiberal and undemocratic features. This chapter distinguishes the five stages of liberal denial.[1]

If you are a "liberal," like me, your Facebook and Twitter feeds are undoubtedly flooded with messages like "make 2016 stop already" and "[insert event] shows that 2016 was the worst year ever." From Brexit to the Berlin attack to the death of George Michael, almost everything seems to fit this overarching narrative: 2016 was exceptionally bad and 2017 will be better – if not bring an outright return to the "normal" state of pre-2016.

These seemingly harmless posts and tweets are illustrations of a deeper psychological process of liberal denial that, in its most extreme form, has profoundly illiberal and undemocratic features. These are the five stages of liberal denial, which political developments like the Brexit referendum and the Trump election have so painfully exposed this year.

30.1 Mockery

The first stage of liberal denial has been ongoing for decades and reflects liberal confidence in itself and the political system. Comfortably in power, populists and other illiberal democrats are mainly mocked for being inarticulate and uninformed; amateurs that barely put a scratch on liberal self-confidence. In fact, they only strengthen it, evidence that *they* are incapable of replacing *us*. Good examples, among many, many more, were Bob Geldof's so-called "Thames flotilla battle" with Nigel Farage or the responses to Trump's Cinco de Mayo tweet (also known as "Taco-Bowl-Gate").

30.2 Outrage

The second stage is that of liberal outrage, which has dominated 2016 around the world – but particularly within liberal circles in the UK and US, which were most shaken by the so-called populist surge. During this stage liberals are still confident about their dominance but are starting to worry about the illiberal challenge. Hence, the outrage is not just addressed toward fellow-liberals but is also meant to shock potential populist supporters into submission. How can anyone support [insert illiberal challenge] given that they do/say [insert illiberal action/statement]? Among the most high-profile moments of liberal outrage surrounded the UKIP "Breaking Point" poster, and the leaked video tape recording of Donald Trump and Billy Bush (see Chapter 20).

30.3 Disbelief

In the third stage of liberal denial *they* have won but *we* don't yet believe it. Liberals try to come up with arguments why the initial results do not really mean the rejection of the liberal position and system. For example, in the UK academics and politicians continue to claim that (Hard) "Brexit is not the will of the British people," while in the US the dominant media narrative is that (white) people didn't vote for Trump's core populist radical right agenda – of nativism, authoritarianism and populism – but merely protested their "economic pain" (see Chapter 16).

30.4 Conspiracies

When it finally has sunk in that the election/referendum has been lost, liberals enter the fourth stage of denial, slowly but steadily accepting that (some of) the voters have actually rejected the liberal consensus. However, still in denial, they argue that it is not a real rejection of liberalism; or, if you wish, not a rejection of real liberalism. No, there are shadowy forces at work here: "fake news" and "propaganda" have created a "post-truth" world. Behind all of this, according to many liberal pundits, is Putin's Russia. From the Dutch referendum on the EU-Ukraine Treaty to the British EU referendum and the US presidential election, Putin has won them all! In the ultimate liberal conspiracy theory, Russia even "hacked" the US presidential election. Ironically, this inspired many liberals to donate a staggering $9.5 million for a recount in swing states to Green candidate Jill Stein, who is a regular on Russia's main disinformation channel, RT.

30.5 Democratic denial

The final, and ultimate, stage of liberal denial is the rejection of the democratic legitimacy of the new political reality. Whether it is because of conspiracy theories or institutional technicalities, liberals argue that the election/referendum outcome is not "democratic" and should therefore be rejected. In Britain some liberals have called for a "second referendum" – in line with a well-established EU tradition to overcome negative referendum outcomes – or for Parliament to reject Brexit – which was even expressed by the European Parliament. In the US the arguments focused primarily on the Electoral College, an indeed undemocratic institution, but largely ignored before Hillary Clinton lost the election.

There is no doubt that 2016 was a bad year for liberals, and liberal denial has not made it any better. Moreover, liberal denial ensures that liberals will be unable to withstand and overcome their consequences in 2017 (and beyond). Before *we* can truly defend liberal democracy, we *must* honestly and openly reflect upon the process of liberal denial, including our own illiberal and undemocratic reflexes. While we should actively reject attacks on the key institutions and values of liberal democracy, as well as their mainstreaming by the media and political establishment, we must do this within those same institutions and values. If we continue to wallow in liberal denial, however, liberal democracy will really be defeated, by *them* and by *us*.

Note

1 This chapter was first published in *Newsweek* (30 December 2016).

31 We are thinking about populism wrong
And it's costing us

Populism has become the political buzzword of the 21st century, but with its increased use comes also increased confusion. The dominance of the populism lens, and its vague usage, make it so we see both too much populism and too little non-populism.[1]

We have to talk about the P-word. It is truly everywhere these days. And everyone is using it: men, women, I even heard some children say it. I'm talking, of course, about populism. You can't read an article about politics these days without it. Virtually any election or referendum is set up as a struggle between an emboldened populism and an embattled establishment. There is no room for anything else.

Don't get me wrong, populism is a useful concept to understand contemporary politics in Europe, and far beyond, but only under two strict conditions. First, it must be clearly defined, and second, it should be applied as one of several concepts to understand politics. Unfortunately, this is not the case in most accounts of politics and populism today. The dominance of the populism lens makes it so we see both too much populism and too little non-populism.

Populism is used in many different ways, mostly devoid of any clear definition, instead broadly referring to irresponsible or untraditional politics, such as promising everything to everyone or speaking in a folksy way. Neither is specific to populism, and both are in fact rather widespread in political campaigning more generally. Instead, populism is best defined as the following: *An ideology that considers society to be ultimately separated into two homogeneous and antagonistic groups – "the pure people" and "the corrupt elite" – and argues that politics should be an expression of the* volonté générale *or general will of the people.* [2]

Populism is both monist and moralist. Populists believe that *all* people share the same interests and values, and that the key distinction between *the* people and *the* elite is moral, i.e. "pure" versus "corrupt."

They present politics as a struggle of all against one, one against all, which, ironically, is confirmed by the dominant media narrative of an emboldened populism versus an embattled establishment.

There is no doubt that populism is an important aspect of contemporary politics; populist parties are represented in most European parliaments and populist presidents and prime ministers rule in both European and American countries. But most of these parties and politicians are not just populists; they combine populism with other ideological features. Left populists combine populism with some form of socialism – think SYRIZA in Greece or Chavismo in Venezuela – while right populists primarily combine it with authoritarianism and nativism – think US President Donald Trump in America or Geert Wilders in the Netherlands.

Before the rise of left populism, right populists would be discussed as "radical right" rather than "populists," while a combination of the two, populist radical right (or, if you wish, radical right populism), is most appropriate. This is not just an academic matter, however. Because Western media tend to perceive the contemporary challenge to liberal democracy exclusively in terms of populism, they focus predominantly on anti-establishment sentiments by political outsiders. Hence, media outlets were quick to celebrate conservative Prime Minister Mark Rutte's victory of "good populism" over Geert Wilders' "bad populism."

What was missed, however, was that the People's Party for Freedom and Democracy (VVD) leader Rutte and Christian Democratic Appeal (CDA) leader Sybrand Buma conducted an increasingly authoritarian and nativist campaign. Both the CDA and VVD presented themselves as defenders of "Christian" and "Dutch values," including the singing of the national anthem and the racist tradition of Black Pete. VVD parliamentary leader Halbe Zijlstra even suggested Easter eggs were under threat from Islam and Muslims, assisted by secular, left-wing fellow travelers. And Rutte took it a step further by explicitly targeting immigrants and refugees in his "act normal" campaign, implying that even descendants of immigrants are at best probationary Dutch citizens.

But whereas most media saw too little in the Dutch elections, they saw too much in the British European Union referendum and the US presidential election. Both are now routinely hailed as populist victories, which is an exaggeration at best and a falsehood at worst. While the UK Independence Party (UKIP) played an important role in pushing the "Leave" camp over the 50 percent mark, the push for Brexit was always predominantly a Conservative endeavor. Hence, many Brits didn't vote *against* some kind of "corrupt elite," be it British or European, but rather *for* re-establishing national sovereignty, as they perceive it, in line with a significant part of the Tory elite.

Similarly, despite all the hype, the 2016 US presidential election was, first and foremost, just another presidential election, in which Republicans voted Republican and Democrats voted Democrat. It might be true that populism motivated some angry white working-class men in the "American heartland" to turn out, which might have swung these states and thereby the whole election, but they constituted at best a tiny minority of the Republican electorate. The vast majority of people who voted for Trump did so for traditional Republican reasons like abortion, immigration, taxes, and, most notably, partisanship.

In short, it is time to put the populism frame back in its correct place. Yes, populism is an important feature of contemporary politics, but not all anti-establishment politics is populism, and populist parties are not just about populism. In fact, to accurately understand politicians like Trump and Wilders, and the challenge they pose to liberal democracy, authoritarianism and nativism are at least as important as populism, if not more so. Moreover, while established politicians mainly adopt populism in their campaign rhetoric, authoritarianism and nativism are actually implemented in their policies, as we can see in recent responses to the refugee crisis and terrorism, from the EU-Turkey deal to the state of emergency in France.

If we want to truly understand contemporary politics, and protect liberal democracy, it is time we focus on all aspects of the populist radical right challenge, including from inside the political establishment, not just on the populism of the outsiders. Because under the cover of fighting off the "populists," the political establishment is slowly but steadily hollowing out the liberal democratic system.

Notes

1 This chapter was first published in the *Huffington Post* (20 March 2017).
2 For a more elaborate discussion of this approach, see Cas Mudde and Cristóbal Rovira Kaltwasser, *Populism: A Very Short Introduction* (Oxford: Oxford University Press, 2017).

32 The Trump presidency
The far right in power?

While it can be convincingly claimed that Donald Trump got elected on the basis of a far right campaign, does that also mean that he rules as a far right president? Even after 100 days, this question is not so easy to answer. The Trump administration is a chaotic beehive of various factions, which are isolated from and opposed to each other, and all vie for the attention of the president.

One hundred days into Donald Trump's presidency we know only one thing for sure: inexperienced and isolated administrators make for a chaotic administration. What the ideological foundation of this chaotic administration is, and will be, remains unclear, however. Except for a lack of political experience, most key people in Trump's new administration seem to have little in common. It is a unique hotchpotch of very diverse groups of largely unconnected individuals: family members, ultra-conservatives, billionaires, generals, and far rightists. Ideologically they disagree on as many issues as they agree upon.

The first group, which seems to be the only one he is truly loyal to, is his direct family. While his sons Eric and Donald Jr. are responsible for the Trump business empire, of which their father has allegedly separated himself, his daughter Ivanka and her husband Jared Kushner play a more prominent political role. Ivanka seems to be the most moderate of all people that surround Trump, having spoken out mainly on concerns related to working women and working mothers. Her husband, with whom Trump not only shares a daughter but also an experience as crown prince to a real estate empire, played a very prominent role in the Trump campaign and is now his senior advisor with allegedly "Rasputin-like power." Kushner is an orthodox Jew with strong ties to Israel who has no previous governmental or political experience. He was one of the few people present during Trump's first phone calls with foreign leaders, including with Russian President Vladimir Putin, and is said to oversee Middle Eastern affairs.

The second group, which is probably the most powerful within the official cabinet, i.e. the official heart of the administration, is that of the ultra-conservatives. They show the crucial role that the ultra-conservative think tank The Heritage Foundation, and particularly its political arm Heritage Action for America, played in the transition process. Heritage is one of the most powerful neoconservative think tanks in the US, but, unlike the larger American Enterprise Institute (AEI), it has a contentious relationship with the GOP establishment. While it never officially endorsed Trump as a candidate, Heritage Action officials met with the Trump camp soon after he clinched the Republican nomination, discussing possible collaboration later. During the transition process The Heritage Foundation advised the inexperienced Trump Team on virtually every policy field. Because of the close ties, CNN (7 December 2016) referred to the organization as "Donald Trump's think tank."

The two most influential representatives of the group of ultra-conservatives with close ties to The Heritage Foundation are Vice-President Mike Pence and Attorney-General Jeff Sessions, two of the few insider-outsiders within the Trump administration. Heritage President Jim DeMint knows Sessions and Pence from his days in the Senate and calls the VP "a great friend." Pence was also an early supporter of the Tea Party and has close ties to the Koch brothers, the most important financial donors of conservative causes in America. As governor of the Midwestern state of Indiana, he mainly gained national attention with his extremist views on traditional social issues. For instance, he pushed through a controversial "religious freedom law" (now also promoted by Trump) and some of the most radical anti-abortion legislation. In fact, many of his signature pieces of legislation were so controversial that his hand-picked successor, fellow Indiana Republican Eric Holcomb, repealed them in his first month in office.

Former Alabama Senator Jeff Sessions also has longstanding relations with Heritage. Unsurprisingly, the think tank called Sessions "the perfect pick," as soon as Trump had announced him as attorney-general. Sessions has a long and troubled history with civil liberties, particularly for African American and Hispanic minorities – the reason why he was not confirmed as a Supreme Court judge in 1986. He twice co-sponsored the English Language Unity Act, which would make English the official language of the United States, has been one of the most outspoken opponents of immigration reform (and particularly any kind of amnesty for undocumented immigrants), and is a harsh critic of the "intrusive" Voting Rights Act of 1965, passed to overcome the legal and practical disenfranchisement of African Americans in the South.

While Trump's Chief of Staff Reince Priebus is not really an ultra-conservative, and is closer to neoliberal House Speaker Paul Ryan than to The Heritage Foundation, as the former chair of the Republican National Committee (RNC), he holds quite strong ties to both Pence and Sessions. It remains to be seen how influential Priebus really is. Many commentators have speculated that Trump chose Priebus because he can bring the GOP on board with the Trump administration, but is too weak to really weigh on Trump. On the other hand, many believe that he was instrumental in forcing General Michael Flynn to resign his position of National Security Advisor (see below).

The second most important group in the cabinet is that of the billionaires, such as Secretary of Commerce Wilbur Ross and Secretary of Education Betsy DeVos, which mainly share significant wealth and a disdain for the (federal) government. In the spirit of Ronald Reagan, they perceive the government as the problem rather than the solution, and call for further deregulation of the economy and privatization of most state services, including education and health care. Almost none of the billionaires has political experience or is directly connected to conservative think tanks. That said, several of them, including DeVos and Secretary of State Rex Tillerson, have (in)direct connections to the American Legislative Exchange Council (ALEC), one of the most effective conservative think tanks, responsible for thousands of laws at the local, state and federal levels.

The third group within the cabinet is constituted by retired generals, most notably Secretary of Defense James "Mad Dog" Mattis and Secretary of Homeland Security John F. Kelly – Trump reached out to several other generals, who for various reasons declined to serve in his administration. While the presence of generals in presidential administrations is not new to the US (think of General Colin Powell who served as Secretary of State under President George W. Bush), no president has appointed so many generals as Trump. While Kelly and Mattis have been reasonably uncontroversial, former General Michael Flynn was a cause of broad concern from the moment he appeared as an advisor to the Trump campaign, already in February 2016. In addition to dubious connections to Putin's Russia and Erdogan's Turkey, Flynn has expressed extremist Islamophobic views, not surprising for a board member of ACT! for America, which the Southern Poverty Law Center (SPLC) classifies as an "anti-Muslim hate group." Flynn was succeeded by another general, the much less controversial Herbert Raymond "H.R." McMaster, who intends to remain on active duty while holding his new governmental position.

His extreme Islamophobia put Flynn close to the last group, which is generally described as the Bannon Group, centered around Trump's alleged other Rasputin, Steve Bannon. Bannon came to prominence when he transformed Breitbart News from a fairly mainstream conservative website into a popular radical right online media empire. Bannon opened Breitbart to all anti-establishment voices on the right, from British gay shock-blogger Milo Yiannopoulos to American "white nationalist" journalist Virginia Hale. While Breitbart regularly panders to the anti-Semitic "alt-right," by using dog-whistles about "globalism" linked to prominent Jews like George Soros, it continues to have many Jewish writers and has a staunchly "pro-Israel" (i.e. pro-Likud and even further right in Israel) Jerusalem platform.

To the surprise of many, Bannon was brought in as chief executive of Trump's presidential campaign in August 2016. He gave Trump's anti-establishment critique a more populist flavor, rebranding the, until then narrow, campaign to elect Trump president, into a "movement" to give power back to the American people. Trump rewarded Bannon by making him White House chief strategist, which makes him one of the closest advisors to the president. Bannon brought in several people with fairly similar ideas, such as "counter-terrorism advisor" Sebastian Gorka, who worked for Breitbart News and Fox News, and "special assistant to the president" Julia Hahn, a former Breitbart News staff writer.

On paper, the far right contingent is the least important, given that none holds a cabinet-level position – undoubtedly in part because that would require confirmation by the US Congress, which Bannon would be unlikely to get. However, what we have learned from the first weeks is that President Trump largely ignores his cabinet and rules by executive order, flanked by a small set of advisors, in particular Bannon and Kushner. For example, Trump has almost completely ignored Secretary of State Tillerson so far, although many of his executive orders, and phone conversations and meetings with foreign leaders, have clear foreign policy consequences.

In fact, the power seems to lie with Bannon, Sessions, and the young Stephen Miller, who links the two veterans. Despite being just 31 years old, "senior policy advisor" Miller has served in Senator Sessions's staff on Capitol Hill for ten years, making him one of the most experienced political operatives in the Trump White House. He also bridges Sessions's more old-fashioned populist Southern nativism with Bannon's more modern populist "economic nationalism." Bannon and Miller were instrumental in pushing through the "Muslim Ban," i.e. the suspension of refugees from seven Muslim-majority countries, and from shielding it from review by other members of the Trump administration and the government. They are also behind the push for a complete overhaul of the US immigration system, which is aimed at significantly limiting non-European immigration.

The far rightists within the Trump administration are distinctly American, having some features that set them apart from contemporary European counterparts. First and foremost, they are proud capitalists, with Bannon even ascribing moral values to the capitalist system. Hence, they share a belief in deregulation and privatization with the billionaires and ultra-conservatives. Similarly, they are religious, although referring mostly to "Judeo-Christian values." In fact, in a speech at the Vatican, at a conference organized by the somewhat secretive Catholic nongovernmental organization, Human Dignity Institute, Bannon argued that "the enlightened capitalism of the Judeo-Christian West" was threatened by a host of evils, including "state-sponsored capitalism," "jihadist Islamic fascism," and "an immense secularization of the West."[1] According to Bannon, secularism "has sapped the strength of the Judeo-Christian West to defend its ideals."

In line with the most extreme Islamophobes in Europe, such as Dutch populist radical right leader Geert Wilders, Bannon believes that the "Judeo-Christian West" is at war with Islam. According to him, the

> Unpleasant fact is that there is a major war brewing, a war that's already global. It's going global in scale, and today's technology, today's media, today's access to weapons of mass destruction, it's going to lead to a global conflict that I believe has to be confronted today. Every day that we refuse to look at this as what it is, and the scale of it, and really the viciousness of it, will be a day where you will rue that we didn't act.

Bannon has also flirted with ideas of the communist Vladimir Ilyich Lenin and the fascist Julius Evola, expressing not just the idea that violence is sometimes necessary to achieve political goals, but that war has a cleansing effect and is therefore good.[2] These are ideas that are only held within largely marginal extreme right *groupuscules* in Europe, mostly within national-revolutionary and neo-Nazi circles.

In short, the first 100 days show that the Trump administration is essentially a radical right government behind an ultra-conservative façade. It has mostly emphasized nativist policies, covered by sharp authoritarian and populist discourse. At the same time, socio-economically, it is pushing for classic neoliberal policies in the domestic arena, while covering this with a discourse of economic nationalism in the foreign arena. Bannon and Miller have proven crucial in drafting the most controversial executive orders in the first weeks, which stood out not just in terms of their nativism but also their amateurism. Once Sessions got involved, the executive orders became barely less nativist, but somewhat more professional. At the same time, Sessions focuses strongly on one of Trump's other obsessions, alleged voter fraud. While there is no evidence that significant voter fraud exists, it provides useful cover for an even more extensive campaign of voter suppression, through introducing voter ID laws and closing places where people can get drivers' licenses or can vote.

This is not to say that the Trump presidency will remain an essentially radical right administration. While the position of Sessions is solid, based largely on the fact that he was the first member of Congress to openly support Trump's candidacy in the primaries, Bannon is much more controversial. He truly is a political outsider and has made his disdain for the Republican establishment very clear. With the exception of Sessions, himself an outsider with relation to the GOP establishment, Bannon has few friends in Trump's inner circle, and allegedly some powerful enemies (notably Priebus and Pence, as well as Ivanka and Jared). Given that the power of most other far rightists rests on Bannon's patronage, with the exception of Sessions's protégée Miller, the (inevitable) fall of Bannon would almost certainly mean the marginalization, although not the disappearance, of the more extreme far right faction. Time will have to tell.

Notes

1 His speech has been reproduced, verbatim, by BuzzFeed. See J. Lester Feder, "This Is How Steve Bannon Sees the Entire World," *BuzzFeed*, 15 November 2016.
2 See also Flemming Rose, "I Told Steven Bannon: 'We Are Not At War With Islam.' He Disagreed," *Huffington Post*, 13 February 2017.

33 What to read on Trump(ism)

To end the book on a positive note, this chapter shortly discusses some of the main scholarship on the far right in America, which will provide interested readers with an (even) better understanding of Trumpism.[1]

In Chapter 18 I criticized US political science for being blind on the right eye, arguing that scholars of American politics have been ill-prepared for three of the main political developments in American politics this century: the role of neoconservatives in the George W. Bush administration, the rise of the Tea Party, and the current success of Donald Trump. I argued that the reasons for this blind spot are of a structural nature, affecting the study of American politics even more than other parts of the discipline.

I ended the post with a promise to provide a list of the limited scholarship that could help provide a better understanding of the rise of Donald Trump and Trumpism, i.e. his unique form of radical right politics (see Chapter 13). I don't claim to include all relevant resources; most notably, I focus exclusively on books (referencing the original and most recent and updated version). Few of these studies have been written by political scientists, let alone by mainstream political scientists, but perhaps the phenomenal public attention paid to Trump will change that (full details of these books are provided in the bibliography).

As I have argued in several other chapters, nativism and radical right politics have a long history in the United States. The classic study to understand the long tradition of American nativism is historian John Higham's seminal *Strangers in the Land: Patterns of American Nativism, 1860–1925* (1955/2002), which covers the period of the Know Nothings to the second coming of the Ku Klux Klan. The classic study of the postwar radical right is sociologist Daniel Bell's edited volume *The Radical Right: The New American Right* (1963/2001), which focuses particularly on the anti-communist radical right of the 1950s, which the progressive historian Richard Hofstadter famously referred to as "the paranoid style in American politics."

There are three books that focus on the whole period of the mid-19th century to the late 20th century. Sociologists Seymour Martin Lipset and Earl Raab's *The Politics of Unreason: Right Wing Extremism in America, 1790–1977* (1970/1978), discusses the US radical right on the basis of a sociological theory of status politics and working-class authoritarianism that is still highly current today. Historian David H. Bennett's *The Party of Fear: The American Far Right from Nativism to the Militia* (1988/1995) is more a "narrative history," which puts individual groups and movements within their specific historical context. In *Right-Wing Populism in America: Too Close for Comfort* (2000) political activists Chip Berlet and Matthew N. Lyons, finally, provide the most comprehensive and detailed overview of the US radical right through the conceptual lens of populism and producerism, tying it somewhat to the much more developed literature on the European radical right.

But to understand the rise of Trump and Trumpism we should not only look at the (often fringe) radical right, or what the media have come to misguidedly call "alt-right" in recent times, but also at the transformation of the two-party system in general, and the Republican Party in particular. In *From the New Deal to the New Right: Race and the Southern Origins of Modern Conservatism* (2009) University of Oregon political scientist Joe Lowndes analyzes the conscious strategy within the Grand Old Party (GOP) to use "race" to force a realignment in the South, where nativist and racist voters had traditionally supported the so-called Dixiecrats. In many ways the Trump campaign can be seen as the extremist swansong of the Southern strategy of the GOP. The bestseller *It's Even Worse Than It Looks: How the American Constitutional System Collided with the New Politics of Extremism* (2012/2016), by think tankers Thomas E. Mann and Norman Ornstein, provides a useful complementary perspective to Lowndes study, focusing more specifically on the radicalization of the GOP in Congress, clearly showing that the GOP was not "hijacked" by Trump, it *created* Trump!

Surprisingly, the rise of the Tea Party, just a few years ago, features little in the current debate on Trump. And yet, as the few insightful studies of the Tea Party show, both phenomena play on very similar attitudes and frustrations. In the most empirical account, *Change They Can't Believe In: The Tea Party and Reactionary Politics in America* (2013), political scientists Christopher S. Parker (University of Washington) and Matt A. Barreto (UCLA) hark back to the theories of the 1960s and 1970s (e.g. Bell and Lipset) as they interpret the Tea Party primarily as a reactionary response to recent changes in American society, most notably related to majority-minority relations. Harvard University political scientists Theda Skocpol and Vanessa Williamson take a different approach in their *The Tea Party: The Remaking of Republican Conservatism* (2013), emphasizing the internal struggles *within* Republican conservatism and the role of the conservative media (notably Fox News). Finally, *Steep: The Precipitous Rise of the Tea Party* (2012) is a highly original volume edited by Lawrence Rosenthal and Christine Trost, who direct the Center for Right-Wing Studies at the University of California at Berkeley, as far as I know the only research center in the US specifically devoted to right-wing politics (full disclosure: I am affiliated with the Center). *Steep* is of particular value because it includes scholars from various disciplines adopting different, and sometimes opposing, theoretical perspectives on the character and explanations of the Tea Party.

But the Tea Party is not the only conservative uprising against the Republicans in name only (RINOs). In a fascinating new book, *Right-Wing Critics of American Conservatism* (2016), University of Alabama political scientist George Hawley presents an overview of the heterogeneous fauna of right-wing groups and individuals that exist in the shadows of the GOP, from libertarians to white supremacists. In his book *Terrified: How Anti-Muslim Fringe Organizations Became Mainstream* (2016) Duke University sociologist Christopher A. Bail focuses on a specific subculture that has been instrumental in bridging the mainstream right and the radical right in the US. The importance of Islamophobia to the 2016 presidential campaign of Trump, as well as some other candidates (like Ted Cruz), is difficult to overstate.

Finally, while there are several specific American aspects to the character and rise of Trump and Trumpism, they are part of a broader rise in radical right politics in Western democracies, most notably in Western Europe. And while the radical right is a fairly marginal topic of study in American politics, it is among the most studied topics in European politics. My own *Populist Radical Right Parties in Europe* (2007) provides a critical "state of the art" overview of the rich scholarship on radical right parties in Europe, while *Revolt on the Right: Explaining for the Radical Right in Britain* (2013), by British political scientists Robert Ford and Matthew J. Goodwin, is an accessible and concise application of the European literature to the British case, specifically the United Kingdom Independence Party (UKIP), perhaps the most familiar to American readers.

Note

1 This chapter was first published in the *Huffington Post* (23 September 2016).

Bibliography

Christopher Bail, *Terrified: How Anti-Muslim Fringe Organizations Became Mainstream* (Princeton, NJ: Princeton University Press, 2016).
Daniel A. Bell (ed.), *The Radical Right: The New American Right* (New York: Anchor Books, 1963).
David H. Bennett, *The Party of Fear: The American Far Right from Nativism to the Militia* (Chapel Hill, NC: University of North Carolina Press, 1988).
Chip Berlet and Matthew N. Lyons, *Right-Wing Populism in America: Too Close for Comfort* (New York: The Guilford Press, 2000).
Marty Cohen, David Karol, Hans Noel and John Zaller, *The Party Decides: Presidential Nominations Before and After Reform* (Chicago, IL: The University of Chicago Press, 2008).
Robert Dahl, *How Democratic is the American Constitution?* (New Haven, CT: Yale University Press, 2003, 2nd edition).
Robert Ford and Matthew J. Goodwin, *Revolt on the Right: Explaining for the Radical Right in Britain* (London: Routledge, 2013).
Francis Fukuyama, *The End of History and The Last Man* (New York: The Free Press, 1992).
George Hawley, *Right-Wing Critics of American Conservatism* (Lawrence, KS: University Press of Kansas, 2016).
Marc J. Hetherington and Jonathan D. Weiler, *Authoritarianism and Polarization in American Politics* (New York: Cambridge University Press, 2009).
John Higham, *Strangers in the Land: Patterns of American Nativism, 1860–1925* (New Brunswick, NJ: Rutgers University Press, 1955).
Piero Ignazi, "The Silent Counter-Revolution: Hypotheses on the Emergence of Extreme Right-Wing Parties in Europe," *European Journal of Political Research*, Vol. 22, No. 1, 1992, pp. 3–34.
Ronald Inglehart, *The Silent Revolution: Changing Values and Political Styles Among Western Publics* (Princeton, NJ: Princeton University Press, 1977).
Seymour Martin Lipset and Earl Raab, *The Politics of Unreason: Right Wing Extremism in America, 1790–1977* (Chicago, IL: The University of Chicago Press, 1978).

Bibliography 127

Joseph E. Lowndes, *From the New Deal to the New Right: Race and the Southern Origins of Modern Conservatism* (New Haven, CT: Yale University Press, 2009).

Peter Mair, *Ruling the Void: The Hollowing of Western Democracy* (London: Verso, 2013).

Thomas E. Mann and Norman Ornstein, *It's Even Worse than it Looks: How the American Constitutional System Collided with the New Politics of Extremism* (New York: Basic Books, 2012).

Nolan McCarty, Keith T. Poole and Howard Rosenthal, *Polarized America: The Dance of Ideology and Unequal Riches* (Cambridge, MA: MIT Press, 2016).

Cas Mudde, "The Populist Zeitgeist," *Government and Opposition*, Vol. 39, No. 4, 2004, pp. 541–563.

Cas Mudde, *Populist Radical Right Parties in Europe* (New York: Cambridge University Press, 2007).

Cas Mudde, "The Rise (and Fall) of American Conservatism," *Journal of Politics*, Vol. 72, No. 2, 2010, pp. 588–594.

Cas Mudde (ed.), *The Populist Radical Right: A Reader* (London: Routledge, 2017).

Cas Mudde and Cristóbal Rovira Kaltwasser, *Populism: A Very Short Introduction* (Oxford: Oxford University Press, 2017).

Christopher S. Parker and Matt A. Barreto, *Change They Can't Believe In: The Tea Party and Reactionary Politics in America* (Princeton, NJ: Princeton University Press, 2013).

Lawrence Rosenthal and Christine Trost (eds), *Steep: The Precipitous Rise of the Tea Party* (Berkeley, CA: The University of California Press, 2012).

Theda Skocpol and Vanessa Williamson, *The Tea Party: The Remaking of Republican Conservatism* (New York: Oxford University Press, 2013).

Ehud Sprinzak, "Right-Wing Terrorism in a Comparative Perspective: The Case of Split Delegitimization," *Terrorism and Political Violence*, Vol. 7, No. 1, 1995, pp. 17–43.

Jusin Vaïsse, *Neoconservatism: The Biography of a Movement* (Cambridge, MA: Harvard University Press, 2011).

Index

Abedin, Huma 29
ACT! for America 119
Akin, Todd 20
Ali, Ayaan Hirshi 30
alt-right 3, 61–3, 68, 84, 120, 124
alternative Right (see alt-right) 62
America First 28, 46, 49
America First Committee 6
America First Party 49
American Enterprise Institute 96, 118
American Independence Party 7
American Legislative Exchange Council (ALEC) 119
American Nazi Party (ANP) 6
American Party (see Know Nothings) 4–5
American Renaissance 61–2
anti-Semitism 2, 27, 29, 61

Bachmann, Michelle 19, 21, 30, 39
Bail, Christopher A. 125
Bannon, Steve 86, 120–22
Barreto, Matt A. 124
Bartels, Larry 94
Bawer, Bruce 12, 30
Bell, Daniel 88, 123–24
Bennett, David H. 124
Berlet, Chip xii, 124
Berlusconi, Silvio 27, 41, 46–8, 51, 66, 86–7, 99
Birtherism 75
Black Lives Matter 44, 63
Black, Don 61
Blee, Kathleen xi, xii
Bloomberg, Michael 38

Bobbio, Norberto 3
Boehner, John 24
Bolton, John 30
Breitbart News 3, 120
Brennan, John 29
Brexit 57–9, 74–7, 82, 84, 111–13, 115,
Brown, Scott 20
Buchanan, Patrick (Pat) 3, 32, 46, 56, 101
Bush, Billy 70–1, 112
Bush, George W. 10, 28–9, 64, 119, 123
Bush, Jeb 40, 44, 68
Butler, Anthea 109

Cain, Herman 19, 30
Caldwell, Christopher 30
Capra, Frank 91
Carson, Ben 41, 106
Center for Security Policy 30
Charen, Mona 28
Christian Right xii, 64
Civil War 5, 23, 80
Clinton, Bill 71, 96
Clinton, Hillary 29, 44, 47, 57, 68, 72, 76, 83–4, 95, 103, 105–6, 113
Cohen, Marty 105
Communist Workers' Party 6
Congress 3, 5, 20, 24–5, 39, 41, 68, 83, 86, 91–2, 96–7, 104, 120, 122, 124
Conservative Political Action Conference (CPAC) 62
Coughlin, Charles Edward "Father" 6, 49
Cruz, Ted 20, 24, 40–4, 56, 68–9, 72–3, 97, 104, 106, 125

D'Souza, Dinish 17
DeMint, Jim 19, 24, 118
Democratic Party 3, 6, 10, 21, 35, 41, 57, 96, 106
Department of Homeland Security (DHS) 13, 18
DeVos, Betsy 119
Diamond, Sara xii
Dixiecrats 3, 6, 101, 124
Drezner, Dan 105
Duke, David 56, 61–2

Erickson, Erick 97
European Union 57, 75, 109, 115
Evola, Julius 121

Fahrenthold, David 70
Fallaci, Oriana 30
Farage, Nigel 77, 83, 108, 111
Federation for American Immigration Reform (FAIR) 7, 90
Fiorina, Carly 32
First Amendment 40, 69
Flynn, Michael 86, 119–20
Forbes, Steve 32
Ford, Henry 50
Ford, Robert 125
Frank, Thomas 101–2
Freedom House 65
FreedomWorks 19, 23
Fukuyama, Francis 28

Gaffney, Frank 29–30
Gatestone Institute 30
Geller, Pamela 29
German American Bund 6
Gingrich, Newt 30, 80, 84
Giuliani, Rudy 80, 84
Global Rally for Humanity 30
Godwin's Law xii
Gohmert, Louie 39, 68, 83
Goldwater, Barry 105
Goodwin, Matthew J. 125
Gore, Al 10
Gorka, Sebastian 120
Grand Old Party (GOP) 19–21, 23–5, 29, 31–3, 36, 39–45, 48–9, 51, 56, 64, 67–73, 77, 84, 86, 95, 97, 99–102, 104–6, 118–19, 122, 124–5

Great Depression 5, 89, 108
Greensboro massacre 6

Hahn, Julia 120
Hale, Virginia 120
Hanley, Sean 71
Hawley, George 125
Head, Tom 16
Heritage Action 24, 86, 118
Heritage Foundation 24, 86, 96, 118–19
Higham, John 123
Hofstadter, Richard 47, 88, 123
Holcomb, Eric 118
Holmes, James Eagan 11
House of Representatives (see Congress) 5, 9, 21, 39, 68
Human Dignity Institute 121

Ignazi, Piero 94–5
Inglehart, Ronald 55, 95
Italian-American Fascist League of North America (FLNA) 6

Jefferson, Thomas 9–10
John Birch Society (JBS) 6, 29, 41, 68, 82
Johnson, Daryl 13

Kardashian, Kim 106
Kasich, John 76, 104
Kazin, Michael xii, 35–6
Kelly, John F. 119
Kelly, Megyn 71
Kerry, John 105
King, Peter 29
King, Steve 7, 39, 68, 83
Klayman, Larry 17
Klingemann, Hans-Dieter 89
Know Nothings 4–5, 33, 49–50, 64, 123
Kobach, Kris 7
Ku Klux Klan (KKK) xi, 5–7, 56, 61, 123
Kushner, Jared 117, 120

Lee, Mike 24
Lenin, Vladimir Ilyich 121
Lincoln, Abraham 10
Lindbergh, Charles A. 6

Lipset, Seymour Martin 88, 124
Long, Huey 46
Lowndes, Joe 124
Lugar, Richard 20
Lyons, Matthew N. 124

Madison, James 9
Maher, Bill 30
Mair, Peter 97
Mann, Thomas E. 96, 124
Mattis, James 119
McCain, John 104–5
McCarthy, Joseph 29
McCarthy, Kevin 67
McConnell, Mitch 40, 67–8
McMaster, Herbert Raymond 119
McVeigh, Timothy 7, 11–12, 18
Militia 7, 12, 15
Miller, Stephen 57, 120, 122
Mourdock, Richard 20
Mussolini, Benito 1

Napolitano, Janet 13
National Alliance (NA) 6, 13
National Policy Institute (NPI) 62
National Socialist German Workers' Party (NSDAP) 6
National Socialist Movement (NSM) 3, 6
National Socialist White People's Party (NSWPP) 6
Native American Party (see Know Nothings) 4
neoconservatism, neoconservatives 1, 28, 63–4, 66, 95–6, 101–2, 118, 123
Nixon, Richard 36–7, 97, 105
Norquist, Grover 43
North Atlantic Treaty Organization (NATO) 28
NumbersUSA 7

Oates, Joyce Carol 30
Obama, Barack 7, 12–17, 19–21, 29, 105
Obamacare 23–5, 32, 36, 41, 67–9
Occupy Wall Street 36, 38, 52–3, 63
Oklahoma City bombing 7, 13, 15, 18
Oregon standoff 45
Ornstein, Norman J. 96, 124

Page, Wade Michael 11
Paine, Thomas 91
paleoconservatives 3, 32, 101
Palin, Sarah 19, 33
Parker, Christopher S. 124
Paul, Rand 19, 100
Paul, Ron 30
Pence, Mike 72, 118–19, 122
People's Party xii, 36
Perot, Ross 7, 32, 36, 48–50
Perry, Rick 30
Pew Research Center 92
Phillips, Melanie 27
Pipes, Daniel 12, 29
Powell, Colin 119
Priebus, Reince 39, 67, 119, 122
Pulitzer, Joseph 55

Raab, Earl 124
Racial Holy War (RaHoWa) 15
Rand, Ayn 20
Reagan, Ronald 17, 28, 37, 95–7, 119
Reform Party 7, 101
Religious Right (see Christian Right) 41
Republican Party (see GOP) 3, 6, 10, 16, 18–19, 21, 35, 39, 41, 43, 57, 67, 75, 81, 83–6, 90, 96–7, 101, 124
Rich, John 91
RINOs (Republicans In Name Only) 97, 125
Rockwell, George Lincoln 6
Romney, Mitt 7, 16, 20–1, 30, 32, 43, 48, 72, 104–5
Rooduijn, Matthijs 54
Roosevelt, Theodore 32
Rosenthal, Lawrence 125
Ross, Wilbur 119
Rove, Karl 20
Rozell, Mark J. 64
Rubio, Marco 19, 21, 41, 44, 69, 76, 97, 104, 106
Ryan, Paul 20, 43, 67, 119

Sanctorum, Rick 30
Sanders, Bernie 35–8, 52–3, 59, 63, 99–100, 106, 109
Sarazin, Thilo 27
Save America Foundation 17
Scarborough, Joe 101
Scheuch, Erwin 89

Second Amendment 7
Senate (see Congress) 20, 40, 67–8, 81, 100, 118
Sessions, Jeff 7, 39, 57, 68, 104, 118–20, 122
Simi, Peter xi
Singh, Guramit 12
Skocpol, Theda 64, 124
Soros, George 120
Southern Poverty Law Center (SPLC) 7, 15, 40, 119
Southern strategy 45, 97, 124
Sowell, Tom 17
Spencer, Richard B. 62
Spencer, Robert 29
Sprinzak, Ehud 17
Stein, Jill 112
Stormfront 12, 15, 61
Supreme Court 84, 105, 118

Tanenhaus, Sam 10
Tanton, John 7
Taylor, Jared 61–2
Tea Party i, xii, 3, 9–10, 16, 18–25, 36–8, 41, 50–1, 53, 63–4, 97, 118, 123–25
Tillerson, Rex 119–20
Trost, Christine 125
Trump, Donald Jr. 117
Trump, Donald, Trumpism i, xi, xii, 3–4, 31–54, 56–9, 62–5, 67–89, 92–109, 111–12, 115–125
Trump, Eric 117
Trump, Ivanka 117, 122

Vaïsse, Justin 64
Vigueri, Richard A. 21

Wallace, George 7, 46, 49–50, 56
Walsh, Joe 21
Warren, Elizabeth 20, 48
WASP (White Anglo-Saxon Protestant) 5, 90
Welch Jr, Robert W. 50
West, Allen 20–1
West, Kanye 106
White House 29, 57, 82, 120,
Wilcox, Clyde xii, 64
Wilders, Geert 12, 27, 32, 44, 56–7, 68, 83, 115–16, 121
Williamson, Vanessa 124

Yglesias, Matthew 31
Yiannopoulos, Milo 120

Zeskind, Leonard xii

Taylor & Francis eBooks

Helping you to choose the right eBooks for your Library

Add Routledge titles to your library's digital collection today. Taylor and Francis ebooks contains over 50,000 titles in the Humanities, Social Sciences, Behavioural Sciences, Built Environment and Law.

Choose from a range of subject packages or create your own!

Benefits for you
- Free MARC records
- COUNTER-compliant usage statistics
- Flexible purchase and pricing options
- All titles DRM-free.

Benefits for your user
- Off-site, anytime access via Athens or referring URL
- Print or copy pages or chapters
- Full content search
- Bookmark, highlight and annotate text
- Access to thousands of pages of quality research at the click of a button.

REQUEST YOUR FREE INSTITUTIONAL TRIAL TODAY

Free Trials Available
We offer free trials to qualifying academic, corporate and government customers.

eCollections – Choose from over 30 subject eCollections, including:

Archaeology	Language Learning
Architecture	Law
Asian Studies	Literature
Business & Management	Media & Communication
Classical Studies	Middle East Studies
Construction	Music
Creative & Media Arts	Philosophy
Criminology & Criminal Justice	Planning
Economics	Politics
Education	Psychology & Mental Health
Energy	Religion
Engineering	Security
English Language & Linguistics	Social Work
Environment & Sustainability	Sociology
Geography	Sport
Health Studies	Theatre & Performance
History	Tourism, Hospitality & Events

For more information, pricing enquiries or to order a free trial, please contact your local sales team:
www.tandfebooks.com/page/sales

Routledge
Taylor & Francis Group

The home of Routledge books

www.tandfebooks.com